ERIC THE SKIER

James B. Kobak, Jr.

Copyright © 2025 by James B. Kobak, Jr.

All rights reserved. No part of this book may be used or reproduced in any manner whatsoever without written permission, except in the case of brief quotations embodied in critical articles or reviews.

Illustrations by James B. Kobak, III

Book layout by HumorOutcasts Press

Published 2025 by HumorOutcasts Press

Printed in the United States of America

ISBN: 979-8-9894863-8-0

Dedication and Acknowledgements

This book is dedicated to my three children and my wife, Carol, all of whom, while being serious citizens of the world, are in my mind imbued with the spirit of Eric and the other characters-- though only very few of their foibles. The book actually originated with stories I made up and told them on long drives to the Adirondacks or other places. All of us are now well into adulthood, but putting the stories into book form recalled many happy memories.

I would especially like to thank my oldest child, Jim, for doing the whimsical illustrations and cover—a far cry from his normal paintings and other artistic endeavors but a great joy to me.

I also want to be sure to acknowledge the insights and suggestion of Kathryn Taylor who helped shape the narrative and of course to Donna Cavanagh and Humor Outcasts Press for helping me turn it into an actual book.

Table of Contents

Eric the Skier 1

Eric's Mother and Father 23

Erika and Her Birch Bark Canoes 29

Alex the Surfer, Eric's Younger Brother 37

Eric's Timid Sister, Edwina 45

Eric The Skier Falls In Love 61

Eric the Skier at the North Pole 73

Eric the Skier and the St. Louis Arch 87

Eric the Skier Goes to the Hospital 105

Edwina and Her Bicycle 115

Edwina's Birthday Surprise 125

Eric the Skier

Eric the Skier skis all year long. He travels around the world on his long, yellow skis following the snow. Eric has a very sensitive nose — a ski jump nose — that can smell a patch of snow from miles away. As the earth warms, it is sometimes harder to find snow than it used to be, but somewhere, somehow, Eric can almost always find some snow that is good for skiing.

Eric the Skier always carries a ton or so of emergency snow in his huge green backpack. If he should come to a bare spot on the slopes, he dumps the snow out of his backpack and rolls over it to smooth it out. Eric is a very strong roller. This is because Eric began rolling at an early age; in fact, the moment he was born, when he rolled off the operating table and started rolling all through the hospital corridors, chased by doctors and nurses who could not run as fast as Eric could roll. When his mother started crying, Eric rolled back to her. He did not want to upset anyone. He just had an urge to roll.

Eric was so good at rolling that he soon grew bored with it. That is how he began to ski. In fact, Eric liked to slide and go downhill so much that he never learned to walk without skis. Even today, Eric almost never takes his skis off except when he is rolling. Then he slides his long yellow skis down the hill and rolls after them.

Eric started to ski when he was even less than one year old. He could do expert trails when he was three. At age four Eric had mastered cross-country skiing and ski jumping. By the time he was five, Eric was winning ski races; the next year he won the Olympics in downhill skiing, cross-country, and slalom. Eric only lost at ski jumping because, still being a child, he thought it more fun to roll down the ski jump than to ski. Eric beat the other skiers in all the other races so easily that he soon grew tired of racing. So Eric started to ski from place to place, inventing new skiing techniques and giving advice to ski instructors.

Skiing from place to place meant that Eric had to leave his family at an early age. This was hard for Eric to do — and even harder for his mother and father and the rest of his family. It also meant that Eric never spent much time in school. But Eric just could not be happy if he was not skiing. Even at school, when he was supposed to be adding, subtracting, or observing scientific experiments, Eric would find himself daydreaming. Then, before he knew it, Eric would find himself on top of his desk, skiing on the erasers or the rulers or his math book. And at recess, when all the other children wanted to trade cards or play freeze tag, all Eric wanted to do was ski.

After he left school, Eric still skied back home from all over the world, even from Australia and Tasmania, several times a year. He sent his parents, brothers, sisters, and teachers, and even the children who played freeze tag, postcards from ski resorts all over the world. Sending the postcards was hard work for Eric. Because he had left school, Eric could not write very well at first and had to practice very hard even to write out a card saying, "Snow is 40" powder base. Wish you were here. Love, Eric." Also, Eric had no money. He had to give ski lessons to pay for the stamps. But Eric always mailed the postcards. He was very kind. He did not want to upset anyone. He just wanted to ski.

Because he did not go to school, there were many things that Eric did not know how to do. He did not know how to tell time from clocks (although from being outdoors so much he learned to tell time from the sun). Eric did not know what a calendar was or what month it was. Of course this was not too important to Eric because Eric always wanted it to be winter. Eric never knew what day of the week it was, or even that different days had different names. Of course for Eric this wasn't too important, either, because for Eric every day was like a Saturday. Eric never knew when his birthday was until his brother and sister reminded him each year. But of course to Eric this also wasn't too important since to Eric every day that there was snow was like the whole world's birthday.

Eric never had much interest in time or history. All he needed to know was that when it was morning he could start to ski and when it was beginning to get dark, it was time to stop. Eric just loved to ski.

There were many other things that Eric never learned to do. He learned to count by counting snowflakes, but he never learned to add or subtract, or to multiply or divide. He didn't know about history or football. He almost never read newspapers, not even the comic strips. He didn't even watch cartoons. Eric did not really have an address or a telephone number, but he wouldn't have known what they were even if he had had them. But Eric knew all there was to know about skiing, and snow, and blizzards.

One thing Eric did learn to do was to read. At first the only words he could read were "E-R-I-C," "S-K-I," "R-E-F-R-E-S-H-M-E-N-T-S," and "E-X-I-T." (Eric had actually learned the word "EXIT" at school because it told him how to get outdoors to where the snow was.) Eric was always getting into trouble because of all the words he could not read. For example, if Eric saw a sign saying

DANGER!

Eric the Skier

GO BACK!

AVALANCHES!

EARTHQUAKES!

GRIZZLY BEARS!

NUCLEAR WASTE DISPOSAL AREA!

he might think it said something like

BEGINNER SKI TRAIL

or

HAVE A NICE DAY

or

FREE PIZZA THIS WAY

or

ROLLING STONES CONCERT

TODAY AT SEVEN O'CLOCK

or anything at all, and down Eric would ski without even putting on his goggles. Luckily, Eric was such a good skier (and so friendly with grizzly bears and other forest creatures) that he never had an accident. But even Eric had some close calls. Sometimes he almost wished he were back home again, rolling around in his mother's kitchen, smelling the oatmeal cookies and all the other good things she was baking.

Before he could read, Eric also used to have a lot of trouble with ski lifts. Because he could not read what the signs said, Eric never knew exactly when to get on or to get off. Sometimes he tried to jump up and get on the ski lift way up near the top, under the sign that said, "Keep Tips Up;" sometimes he jumped off the lift down near the bottom, under the sign saying, "Lower Safety Bar. " Eric once got off the ski lift under the sign saying, "Prepare to Unload" and landed on a huge, jagged rock; another time he jumped off at a sign saying, "Scenic Waterfall" and fell into an icy brook. Still other times Eric could not tell which sign said, "Get Off Here" and stayed on the ski lift for most of the day. Luckily, Eric was such a good skier that he never got hurt when he got off at the wrong place. But it was awfully embarrassing the way everyone else sat in the ski lift and stared at him.

So one day, when Eric was about nine, or eleven, or eight, or thirteen (there is no way of knowing since Eric never kept track of his age), Eric decided to learn how to read. Eric had no books, so he had to gather whatever reading matter he could find at ski lodges: lift tickets, brochures for condominium developments, and skiing magazines. The things Eric gathered to read were also in many different languages since

Eric the Skier

Eric skied all over the world. So Eric learned to read a lot of simple words — words like "A-N-D" and "B-U-T" and "I-T" and "F-O-R" and "T-H-E" and "E-N-T-R-A-N-C-E" (Eric liked this word a lot because it sort of balanced out the word "EXIT" that he had learned at school) — as well as many harder, more complicated worlds that had to do with skiing — words like "K-L-I-S-T-E-R" and "I-N-T-E-R-M-E-D-I-A-T-E" and "P-A-R-A-L-L-E-L" and "R-O-S-S-I-G-N-O-L" and "T-I-M-E-S-H-A-R-I-N-G." Eric learned these words in many languages: English, French, Italian, German, Swedish, Spanish, even Japanese and Czech. Eric learned a little bit of the language of every country having a ski center with brochures. There were many words and phrases that Eric did not learn, words such as "L-I-G-H-T B-U-L-B" and "S-A-L-A-D" and "C-U-P" and "S-A-U-C-E-R" and "S-E-S-A-M-E S-T-R-E-E T." But these were words and phrases that seldom came up in skiing, so Eric did not need to use them very often.

It was hard work learning to read. Eric had no teacher and had to puzzle out the sounds all by himself. He never did figure out the silent "e" at the end of many words in the English language. Even today he thinks a "PINE TREE" is a "PIN TREE," a "FINE DAY OF SKIING" is a "FIN DAY FOR SKIING,' and a "WIPE OUT" is a WIP OUT." Eric still wonders why he has never seen a fish on a "FIN DAY FOR SKIING."

Eric worked hard at his reading. He found he could concentrate best when he was reading while skiing. Eric is one of the few people who can read and ski at the same time. Sometimes people leave books behind at the ski lodge, and Eric will try to read them while he is skiing. Eric has now read many classic works of literature in several languages: Dickens, Shakespeare, Mark Twain, and Samuel Becket; Dostoyevsky and Chekov; Moliere and Victor Hugo: in short, the assigned reading of every college freshman in the northeastern United States. He has read even more love stories, mysteries, and science fiction books, since these are the books most people bring to ski resorts. Eric has also read the autobiography of Lee Iacocca, the traveler's airline guide, the guides to back country inns in Vermont, Maine, and Massachusetts, several dozen cookbooks, six books on how to make money in the stock market, four books on how to make money in real estate, and two books on how to make money in antiquing and automobile mechanics.

Of course Eric does not understand some of these books too well since they use many non-skiing words which he does not know. For example, he sometimes thinks the airplane guide is modern poetry and vice versa. Nevertheless, Eric loves to read these books and memorizes some of them to recite while he is skiing. Actually Eric is one of the few people who can ski, recite Paradise Lost from memory and read the autobiography of Madonna, all at the same time. Eric especially enjoys literature with a lot of snow in it, such as The Magic Mountain or War and Peace or The Call of the Wild. But Eric's favorite book is Huckleberry Finn because, although there is not even one inch of snow in the whole book, it is about having freedom.

Eric the Skier

Even though he does not understand or even pronounce correctly all the words, Eric likes poetry because it has rhythms that remind him of different types of skiing. Also, as Eric reads down a poem he encounters different sights, sounds, and smells, just as he does when skiing down a hill.

Sometimes Eric even listens to poetry on his iPhone. He was given the iPhone for teaching a rock band named Charmed Quark and the Four Neutrinos how to ski on their guitars at St. Moritz. Eric is one of the few people who can ski, listen to one poem, read a second poem, and recite yet a third poem, all at the same time and all in different languages. Eric does not do this too often lest he wear out the memory on his phone, but it is quite a sight when he does. Also quite a sound, since Eric recites quite loudly and mispronounces any word with a silent "e."

Eric loves to discuss the books he has read. Having a conversation with Eric about anything but skiing is not easy, however. Eric's vocabulary consists almost entirely of skiing phrases in different languages. These can be confusing enough when Eric is discussing a good patch of skiing snow, but they become forbidding indeed when Eric applies them to Moby Dick or the cantos of Ezra Pound, especially as Eric talks faster the more difficult the subjects he is discussing, much as he skis faster the steeper the slope of the terrain. Eric's discussion of a book is almost as hard to follow as that of a modern literature professor. It is also a good deal more dangerous since Eric waves his ski poles in the air to emphasize his points, especially his favorite point about transcendentalism and the harpooning of Moby Dick. When Eric has been doing a lot of reading, he — and everyone else — is usually happiest when Eric is off on a remote expert slope, glissading gracefully to messengers' speeches from Shakespearean plays.

When Eric first got his iPhone, he tried to ski to music, as he had seen many other skiers do. But he never really liked it that much. It was hard to listen to Charmed Quark and the Four Neutrinos and concentrate on skiing. Their music consisted of banging their guitars against each other, then banging the guitars against the drum, and then banging the drummer against the guitars. This wasn't the way Eric liked to ski, even during an avalanche.

For a while Eric tried skiing to opera music. Some of the overtures were good for skiing, but then, just as Eric got to the glaciers at Banff or the powder at Aspen, the opera would begin. Eric found it hard to ski to the actual opera. Eric would have to jump high in the air when the soprano sang, then suddenly crouch down low in a tuck when the bass came in, then suddenly do a lot of complicated tricks when someone started singing, "Figaro, Figaro, Figaro." Then when everyone started singing all at once, Eric did not know what to do. Also Eric could never find enough moguls for all the times characters were cursed and kettledrums struck in Italian operas. Not even the Italian Alps had enough moguls.

Eric the Skier

Of course, most of the time when he was skiing, Eric did not listen to anything, or say anything, or read anything at all. Most of the time Eric just skied — skied and looked at the view, skied and listened to the wind and whatever little birds were brave enough to sing through the winter, skied and felt the sun on his face and the slope of the hills in his legs. Most of the time Eric found this the best poetry and music of all.

Eric seldom spends more than a day at any one ski slope. Usually he arrives early in the morning, before the lifts are even open, and leaves a little after lunch — or possibly, if he eats a big lunch, Eric might have a little nap and then leave. Or possibly, if Eric eats an especially large lunch with extra tacos, Eric's little nap might become a big nap (complete with snoring), and Eric might still be yawning when he finally boards the last ski lift of the day.

People at the ski resorts are always happy to see Eric. He tells them the news about their friends at other ski resorts around the world. Then he tells them about new ski techniques that he has invented. Eric gives the ski instructors lessons. If a skier is injured, Eric treats them because he knows all there is to know about skiing first aid. If a ski slope is in disrepair, Eric fixes that, too, taking a thousand pounds or so of snow out of his backpack and rolling over it while singing "Let It Snow, Let It Snow, Let It Snow."

If a child or beginning skier is having trouble managing the skis, Eric gives that skier a lesson. Eric is the world's best ski instructor. When talking about skiing, unlike literature, Eric talks slowly and patiently, and makes hard things seem very simple, like Robert Frost. No matter what the weather, Eric always begins the lesson by saying, "It's a fin day for skiing." Then he tells the beginning skier to practice and never give up. Within half an hour Eric can turn a beginning skier into an expert.

Eric's pupils must give Eric three things: forty-seven cents, one half of a chocolate bar, and one magic word. The forty-seven cents are so Eric can save enough money to buy stamps for his postcards. The half a chocolate bar is for Eric's dessert. The one magic word is "Thank you," and that is to make Eric feel good.

Because of all the work he does, the people at the ski resorts are happy to take care of Eric as long as he cares to stay. They give him breakfast and lunch and supper in a brown paper bag to take with him when he skis to the next resort and all the cocoa he can drink — which is quite a lot of cocoa. Often the owners of the ski resort will ask Eric to spend the night, or a weekend, or a holiday like George Washington's birthday, or the winter, or the rest of his life. But Eric always refuses, saying, "Zankyou. You are too kind. You have a wonderful ski lodge here. It is a fin place for skiing. Ze pin trees and ze cocoa are especially nice. But I have miles to go before I sleep. Zankyou again, sayonara, au revoir, and exit." Of course after Eric leaves, he always writes a nice thank-you postcard saying, "Zankyou for a good time. I am sorry I could not stay. I don't want to upset anyone. I just want to ski." The owners of

Eric the Skier

ski resorts frame these postcards, and many are hanging in museums today.

Eric gets so much exercise that he is an excellent eater. Eric is an adventurous eater, as is his father, and likes foods from the various parts of the world he has visited. For breakfast Eric usually eats twelve pancakes covered with chili, a large glass of grapefruit juice, and fortune cookies. And of course lots of cocoa to wash it all down. At lunchtime Eric has a steaming bowl of French-style split pea soup, some pepperoni, and side orders of tacos and burritos. And of course lots of cocoa to wash it all down. Then for dinner, Eric's brown paper bag will be packed with croissants, sushi, pretzels, gouda cheese, and half a chocolate bar for dessert. And of course a few large thermoses of cocoa to wash it all down.

To tell the truth, Eric never eats the sushi, but is too polite to say he does not like it. Eric usually leaves it near caves in the woods, so the hibernating bears will have something to look forward to when they wake up from their naps. Eric, who eats almost as much as a bear, knows how hungry he feels after one of his afternoon naps! Eric just could never learn to eat any kind of seafood. Eric gets sick to his stomach looking at something that used to live in the water because water makes him think of melting snow, which is something so sad that Eric cannot bear to think about it, least of all when he is eating.

Since Eric can almost always eat his meals at ski lodges, he does not need to carry much other food with him. This is fortunate because with all the snow in his backpack Eric has little extra room. Eric always carries dried grains and fruits in the pockets of his ski pants. Eric sometimes nibbles on these if he is hungrier than usual, but he really brings them along to give to the starving deer he sometimes meets when skiing through the wilderness.

At first the deer and other forest creatures were scared of Eric, but he spent so much time skiing through the wilderness, and moved so gracefully, that gradually they learned to accept him. Then Eric would bring the deer nuts and berries from places where the snow was not so deep. And the deer and the bear would show Eric where to find plants to eat even in the deepest snow, and where to find caves and shelters. So Eric never has to worry if he has to spend a few nights in the woods because of severe avalanches or, as Eric has noticed happening more and more, unexpected warm weather that melts the snow.

Eric taught the deer how to play freeze tag. That is why you see deer standing as still as statutes sometimes and running away so quickly other times. He read William Faulkner's story "The Bear" to the bears. He read Bambi, and Windsor Forest and Watership Down to the other animals in the forest. Sometimes Eric tried to discuss these poems and stories with the animals, but since they didn't really understand language, the discussion was pretty much all Eric and his ski poles, with an occasional chirp or snort from the listeners — much like a poetry reading.

Eric the Skier

Then again, given Eric's use of language, the discussions weren't too different from his discussions with people.

Eric does not carry much other food with him. He always carries a bag of juicy blueberries that his sister Erika has picked for him in a sunny spot at the top of a mountain. He also brings along some of the oatmeal cookies with raisins and walnuts that his mother sends to him at ski resorts around the world. Sometimes, if Eric is travelling an extra-long distance, he might bring along some emergency pepperoni.

Eric also always carries two moldy Van Houten chocolate bars in his backpack. These are a kind of candy bar no longer made but which Eric had taken with him in his school lunch box. Eric never really expects to eat these two old candy bars, which have become as hard as glaciers and are covered with molds as colorful as an Alpine meadow. Eric really carries them around for sentimental reasons because they remind him of his childhood. Of course if Eric is reading at the time, he will stuff the Aeneid, or The Fall of the House of Usher, or a Killington ski brochure or "How to Make Big Money in Small Harpsichords" or whatever else he is reading into his backpack, wrapping it in a tarpaulin so that it will not get wet from the snow.

Eric does not pack equipment for fixing his skis. Eric always skis in such control that he has never broken a pair of skis. Eric does occasionally break a ski pole if he is skiing down Mt. Rainer or K-2 during blizzards, but Eric knows about a secret swarm of bees. These are special bees that live in a secret meadow. They sound like skiers when they fly and even look a little like skis when they fold up their wings and go to sleep at night. The bees make a special beehive out of a special wax. When Eric heats this wax to just the right temperature, it can hold anything together. Eric uses this magic beeswax to fix his broken ski poles.

This magic beeswax is so special that by heating it to just the right temperature, or sometimes not heating it at all, Eric can use it for many different things. For instance, Eric can always wax his skis so they are just right for any kind of snow. That is one reason Eric can ski thousands and thousands of miles year after year on the same pair of skis. Eric can also use the wax to keep his boots and clothes and tarpaulin waterproof. On sunny days Eric can use the wax as suntan lotion. When he is hungrier than he expected to be, Eric can eat the wax like honey. And the wax is also useful for making sure that the stamps Eric buys actually stick to the postcards and thank-you notes Eric is always mailing.

By now Eric has been skiing so long in the wilderness that he knows the way from place to place by heart, just the way most people know the way from the television room to the refrigerator or the cookie jar. Of course, Eric is a good deal thinner than these other people.

Eric can ski so fast because his skis are extra-long — 315 centimeters — and are always waxed just perfectly with magic beeswax from the meadow with the secret swarm of ski bees. Eric can ski downhill or slalom on his long yellow skis; he can ski cross-country and do

Eric the Skier

telemarks on them; he can jump with them, do tricks with them, and even do aerobic dancing routines with them when visiting his mother. Of course, to anyone else the skis would be as slippery as two twelve-foot long banana peels, and skiing on them would be like riding a roller coaster into the side of a skyscraper. But not to Eric. To Eric the skis are easier to control than his own feet.

Eric's extra-long skis are yellow. At first Eric painted his long skis his favorite color, white, the color of snow. But the skis were so long Eric could never tell where they ended and the snow began. Sometimes Eric found himself skiing off cliffs because what he thought was snow off in the distance was actually the tips of his own long skis. In fact, this was how Eric finally learned how to ski jump.

So after a few involuntary jumps, Eric gave the skis to his younger brother, Alex, to paint. Alex painted them yellow, the brightest yellow he could find, a yellow almost as bright as the sun. That way Eric would always be able to see his ski tips off in the distance, even in fogs and snowstorms. Yellow soon became Eric's second favorite color.

On the bottoms, Eric's skis say,

HAVE A FIN DAY.

THESE SKIS BELONG TO ERIC THE SKIER

S.p.A., GmbH, PATENT PENDING.

NO TRESPASSING, VIOLATORS WILL BE PROSECUTED.

Eric has no idea what most of these words mean, but they are interesting phrases he has come across in signs and brochures during his travels around the world.

Eric's ski poles are brown. Eric made them out of twigs and branches. They have sharp points on the bottoms because Eric uses them to spear any litter he sees on the trail. As a child, Eric was not always too neat. He often rolled on paper towels and old Christmas wrapping paper just for the fun of it. But he cannot stand seeing litter in the forest. To him the forest is like a church and a museum all rolled up in one. The forest is a beautiful place. Eric works as hard as he can to keep it that way forever. The forest is good for Eric. And Eric tries to be good for the forest.

Eric cannot always ski from ski center to ski center. Sometimes lakes or oceans or jungles or deserts or airports or cities or continents like Africa are in the way. Then Eric has to take some other form of transportation such as a taxi. Of course Eric cannot usually sit in the taxi, unless it is a stretch limousine, because his skis are too long. Instead, Eric stands on the top with his skis strapped to the ski rack. These taxi rides work fine as long as there are no tunnels on the route.

Eric the Skier

Large bodies of water present a special problem for Eric. Water, you will remember, always makes Eric nervous and depressed because it reminds him of melted snow.

The only way Eric can get from America to Europe is to wait for his sister Erika to come by with her canoe. Then Eric blindfolds himself, and his sister Erika either paddles him all the way across or lets him off at the nearest large iceberg. Even with Erika paddling, Eric is so frightened that he often trembles, making the canoe extremely tippy. But Erika is such a good canoeist that she and Eric always make it across the ocean.

Every few years Eric's brother, Alex, comes by and water skis behind the canoe. Then the three of them reminisce about surveying trips with their father or the old doo-wop songs to which their mother used to teach aerobic dancing. At the end of the trip they all send a postcard to their timid sister, Edwina.

Of course a problem Eric is encountering more and more is unexpected warm weather. Sudden thaws cause all the snow in his huge backpack to start melting, making Eric and everything he owns very wet. The only way to prevent this from happening is for Eric to put the backpack in the huge freezer of a meat packing plant for twelve hours. So whenever Eric feels the first few drips from his pack, he skis to the nearest railroad depot and grabs the caboose of the first train heading west. In the old days, Eric only had to ski behind a train once or twice a year from places a few miles south of Milwaukee or Chicago, but now, with global warming, Eric has to ski behind trains once or twice a month from almost anywhere.

Skiing behind a train would be impossible for anyone else, and even if someone else could do it, their skis would break and all their teeth would fall out from skiing ninety miles an hour over four million railroad ties. To Eric, however, skiing this hard and this fast is not too different from the way he skies down the Matterhorn or Mount Everest. Eric finds it good practice. In fact, to Eric it is quite relaxing since he never has to make any turns. Eric catches up on a lot of his reading during these trips. To keep his skis from breaking, Eric puts an extra layer of his special beeswax on each ski whenever the train stops to drop off mail or take on new freight. By the end of the trip Eric's skis are even stronger and more yellow than usual. So if you ever hear an especially loud train rumbling off in the distance, look down the tracks toward the caboose. All that noise just might be the clattering of Eric's long yellow skis. And you just might catch a glimpse of Eric speeding west, reading speeches by Theodore Roosevelt while water spills out of his backpack.

Eric has a tiny wooden cabin in the woods. He built it himself, with some help one November weekend from his sister, Erika. It has a stove, a sink, a dishwasher, a bathroom, a big wooden bed long enough for Eric to sleep in with his skis on, pots and pans hanging from the ceiling, and lots of brochures from ski resorts. Of course Eric's cabin has no table because it is a tiny cabin, and the bed takes up too much room. There is a

Eric the Skier

big picture window in the front so Eric can see miles and miles of snow when he is falling asleep and as soon as he wakes up in the morning.

No one knows where Eric's cabin is. No one except Eric and Erika has ever seen it, not even Paul Bunyan. Some people think it is in Alaska; others say it is on Mount Everest; others swear it could only be in the Alps, or the Dolomites, or Utah, or Wyoming or Colorado; and a few people suggest it might be nestled against a pretty little mountain named Porter in the Adirondacks. But no one really knows because no one except Eric and Erika has ever been there.

All anyone else knows is that Eric's cabin is the most beautiful place in the world. Eric's cabin is warm and cheerful. The weather is always good. It is always quiet. It is always, as Eric would put it, a "fin day for skiing" there.

So next time you go skiing and the sun is high in the sky and it isn't too cold and the sky is so blue that heaven seems to weep, go off to the side of the trail and stand perfectly still. Squint your eyes so tight that they are just about closed and concentrate as hard as you can. Then concentrate even harder. Concentrate as hard as Eric trying to learn how to read. Then maybe — just maybe — off in the distance you will see the sun shining on Eric's tiny, secret cabin in the woods. Maybe you will even see Eric skiing out the front door, with his huge pack brimming over with brand new snow and the sun gleaming on his long yellow skis. Maybe you will even hear him talking to his friends, the deer. "I don't want to upset anyone," you might hear Eric say, "I just want to ski."

Eric's Mother and Father

Eric's father was a surveyor. He was always going on trips to survey things outdoors. Eric's father took Eric on many of his trips, especially in the winter. That is how Eric learned to use a map and compass.

Once or twice Eric's father took Eric surveying in the spring and summer, but unless there was snow around, Eric soon lost interest and started rolling over things -- including his father, who was carefully setting up his surveying equipment. So when the weather turned warm Eric's father usually left Eric home, rolling around in the kitchen, and took Alex, Erika or Edwina with him instead. But Alex got bored unless Eric's father was surveying something wet, and Erika got bored unless he was surveying something steep. Edwina just worried about whatever it was her father was surveying. Since Eric's father spent most of his time surveying parking lots and baseball fields, he spent most of his time surveying by himself.

Eric's father loved to survey. By the time Eric left home his father had already surveyed half the vacant lots in North America and most of its shopping malls, condominiums, and baseball stadiums.

Eric's father even surveyed around home for fun. He surveyed the garage, the flower beds, the kitchen table, even the doll's houses that Eric's sisters, Erika and Edwina, had as children. Eric's father surveyed the living room on two hundred sixty-three Saturday evenings in a row. This sometimes made Eric's mother angry. She liked going to a movie or a concert every three years or so. She also wasn't too fond of having surveyors' chains all over the couches.

The only thing Eric's father never surveyed was a golf course. Eric's father did not believe in golf. He did not even believe in Jack Nicklaus. Eric's father did, however, survey thousands of tennis courts. Unfortunately, Eric's father had a habit of surveying tennis courts during tennis games, even tennis games in which he was playing. This made him very unpopular with his doubles partners, and he was seldom asked to survey the same tennis court twice.

No matter where he happened to be surveying, Eric's father always stopped surveying for lunch at precisely 12:35 p.m. Eastern Standard

Eric the Skier

Time. (Surveying all the time made Eric's father a very precise person.) Eric's father always ate lunch on top of a nearby hill or mountain. He loved to eat lunch while sitting on a rock with a view that went on for miles. He could see new things that needed to be surveyed spread out before him in every direction.

Eric's father always brought a big lunch with him because he worked so hard at his surveying. He always brought along one food he had never eaten before because he believed in trying new foods. "Here, Eric, try some of this gazpacho," Eric's father would say, handing Eric a bowl of soup. Or, "Here, Eric, try a squid sandwich on toasted rye with lettuce and mayo," he would say, handing his son a squishy package in waxed paper.

"No zankyou, father," Eric would say, feeling sick to his stomach. The squid only made him think of how much of the world was covered by seas and oceans — in other words, melted snow.

"Look over here, Eric," Eric's father would say. "I bet that lake has never been surveyed."

"Yes, father," Eric would say. But the lake, being water, made Eric sad and what Eric was really daydreaming about was what it would be like to ski down the hill behind the lake.

Eric's mother was a gourmet cook and an aerobics dancing instructor. She cooked in the mornings when her kitchen was sunny. Then she danced all afternoon, when it got cloudy. In the evenings, Eric's mother went to meetings. Eric's mother did not actually belong to the organizations that held the meetings. She just liked going to them. It was more interesting than watching TV or surveying the bathtub with Eric's father for the two thousandth time. No one ever minded when Eric's mother came to a meeting uninvited because she always brought refreshments.

Eric's mother gained five pounds every morning from all the nibbling she did of the delicious things she cooked. But Eric's mother danced so hard every afternoon that she never got fat. In fact, she always weighed exactly the same amount: 115 pounds. By coincidence this is precisely the weight of Eric's yellow skis, of Erika's longest birch bark canoe, of Alex's favorite surfboard, and of the gray comforter under which their timid sister Edwina hides every Fourth of July. Once in a while, if Eric's mother should happen to be cooking something like lasagna or lemon meringue pie a la mode, she might gain six or seven pounds. Then she would have to dance extra hard in the afternoon, doing ballet steps and tap dances between her aerobic dancing steps.

Eric used to love rolling around in the sunny kitchen while his mother cooked. She always made Eric a dozen oatmeal cookies with raisins or pieces of chocolate or some other special treat inside them.

Eric's mother still bakes oatmeal cookies with surprises in them for Eric. She sends boxes of oatmeal cookies to ski centers for Eric to pick up whenever he happens to ski by. After sharing the cookies with the other people at the ski center, Eric always puts a few in his backpack in case of emergencies. Eric considers being hungry for more than about ten minutes an emergency.

Every once in a while, Eric's mother would get so excited about a meat loaf or ragout that she was cooking that she would start dancing while cooking. Then anything might happen. She might mistakenly include peppers or pieces of parsley or tomatoes in the oatmeal cookies during a cha-cha; or she might put gumdrops in the stew during a waltz or a foxtrot. Then the people at the meetings she went to would say things like, "Wherever did you find this recipe?" And people at ski centers to whom Eric gave oatmeal cookies would say, "No, thank you, I get motion sickness on the T-bar." But usually what people said were things like "Yum" and "Delicious" and "Yes, thank you, maybe I should try just one more little one since I do plan an extra-long run this afternoon."

Everyone in the family was healthy and had especially strong legs because of all the aerobic workouts they had as children. Although it may be hard to believe, even Edwina is actually strong and healthy — but of course she worries all the time that she isn't. No one could worry as much as Edwina does and not get dreadfully ill unless she were strong and healthy to begin with. And Edwina never actually did the aerobic dancing. Eric's mother was such a vigorous dancer that Edwina got healthy simply by watching. This, in fact, was the philosophy of most of Eric's mother's students.

But not of Eric and his father. When Eric and his father go for their annual physical checkup, which they always do together on one of Eric's visits home, the doctor is always amazed that they are both in such perfect health.

"I am amazed you are in such perfect health," says the doctor.

"Thank you very much," says Eric's father. "Have you had your waiting room surveyed recently?"

"Zankyou very much," says Eric. "It's a fin day for skiing."

"Speaking of skiing," says the doctor, "I noticed Eric still has his skis on. They made his feet look somewhat abnormal in the X-rays. I suppose they are what hit me in the shins when I hit Eric's knee with my hammer to test his reflexes."

"Eric has always had very good reflexes," says Eric's father.

"Yes, I know," says the doctor, "and very strong legs."

"I hope you will understand," Eric's father explains to the doctor as Eric skis through the waiting room, handing out oatmeal cookies. "Eric does not want to upset anyone. He just wants to ski."

Erika and Her Birch Bark Canoes

As much as Eric loves winter, his sister, Erika, loves the spring and fall; as much as Eric loves snow, Erika loves blueberries. Erika spends the year canoeing and hiking — canoeing and hiking and gathering blueberries.

Erika hikes and canoes during the spring and fall in the same places Eric skis in the winter. She even spends a few days every October and May in Eric's secret wooden cabin in the woods. Erika is the only person in the world besides Eric who has ever seen Eric's cabin. Erika helped Eric build the cabin one November weekend. After she stays in the cabin, Erika always gives it a thorough cleaning with a broom made out of pine boughs. Then she washes the pots and leaves a large supply of firewood and finally writes a thank-you note in blueberry ink and leaves a basketful of fresh blueberries in the refrigerator.

Erika hikes and hikes until she comes to a brook that is exactly as wide as Erika is tall — five feet, two inches. Then Erika makes a tiny birch bark canoe and a tiny birch wood paddle and paddles downstream as far as the water will take her. Erika can paddle her tiny birch bark canoes through anything; rapids and whirlpools are no obstacle for her. Even waterfalls don't stop Erika; she just has to pay extra attention. Erika often paddles through underground grottoes and caves that no one else has ever seen, not even her brother, Eric.

When Erika canoes downstream, the little brook turns into a big brook, which turns into a little river, which turns into a big river, which turns into a great river. Then Erika finds herself at the oceanside. She waits there to see if the weather is turning cold or if Eric needs a ride across the ocean.

Erika uses an especially large canoe with an especially large paddle when she canoes Eric across the ocean. The canoe has to be especially large or Eric could not fit into it with his skis. While she is canoeing across the ocean in her large canoe, Erika hides the tiny birch bark canoe and tiny birch wood paddle she has made in marshes and wetlands, places where other people never go, places where snowy egrets use the canoes as nests.

Eric the Skier

When Erika reaches shore after canoeing across the ocean, she says goodbye to Eric, gives him a fresh supply of blueberries, and hikes and hikes uphill again until she comes to another brook that is exactly five feet, two inches wide. Then she builds another tiny birch bark canoe and another tiny birch wood paddle and paddles back down. Erika loves to hike uphill because she finds blueberries along the way. But she likes to canoe back down and eat the blueberries even more.

Erika never gets lost when hiking and canoeing any more than Eric does when he goes skiing. Erika knows many secret trails. She knows the way to hundreds of fire towers in the woods, even some that have been abandoned and everyone else has forgotten. On her way to find a brook to canoe down, she likes to climb up any fire tower nearby and talk to the forest ranger, if one is on duty. She will give the ranger blueberries as they look for forest fires and talk between munches of berry about why there seem to be more fires and storms each year as the world gets warmer. These are things Erika worries about not only for herself but for all the people who need and enjoy them, and even for her friends, the birds. Erika is as sad about thinking about disappearing forests or seeing damaged trees as Eric is about melting snow.

Erika is as friendly with birds as Eric is with deer and other forest creatures. The same birds sometimes fly around Erika for years at a time since they always go south in the fall and north in the spring, just as Erika does. There are hundreds and hundreds of these birds. Birds of all kinds and many different colors. Erika knows the names of all of them, just as girls remember the names of all their dolls.

Erika does not play freeze tag with the birds as Eric does with the deer because Erika cannot fly. Anyway, the birds would fall down and hurt themselves if they had to freeze in midair. So Erika has singing contests with the birds instead. If you should ever hear a sparrow that sounds like Montserrat Caballe or Tina Turner, you can rest assured that it is a sparrow that has spent some time flying alongside Erika and her birch bark canoe.

Erika loves music and singing. Sometimes at night, if she is lonely, as she sometimes is, Erika makes tiny guitars and miniature violins out of birch bark and pine boughs and plays chamber music by herself. The only music Erika does not like is Wagnerian opera. That is because Erika can sing better than any of the sopranos — and louder than any of the orchestras.

Erika paddles her tiny birch bark canoes down cascades and waterfalls in time to music. It is quite something to see Erika bobbing along the Ohio River to Beethoven's Third Symphony or floating through rapids on the Rappahannock to the strains of Rimsky-Korsakoff's "Scheherazade." But most of all Erika likes to j-stroke to "The Magic Flute." That is the prettiest sight of all — Erika paddling down the Danube in a tiny canoe, whistling the parts of Papageno and Papagena, as

Eric the Skier

thousands of birds fly behind her and her long blond hair spreads like a banner on the wind.

Erika carries a large green backpack. It is only slightly smaller than Eric's. Erika puts into her backpack almost exactly the same things that Eric puts into his, except that Erika always packs a wedding dress, just in case she should want to get married and Paul Bunyan or Johnny Appleseed should come along. Also, in the part of the backpack in which Eric always packs his emergency snow, Erika always packs blueberries, tens of thousands of sun-ripened blueberries picked from secret places on cliff ledge and mountainsides.

Erika sends the blueberries to her parents, her sister, Edwina, and her brother, Alex. "Products of nature. Handle with care," she writes on the package. She always leaves a fresh supply of blueberries in Eric's refrigerator in his secret cabin in the woods. Erika squeezes blueberries and uses the juice as syrup for the pancakes she sometimes makes for her breakfast when she is facing a long hike. For lunch, Erika eats blueberry sandwiches. For dinner she makes a salad by mixing blueberries with dandelions, wildflowers, and herbs and spices which Erika picks in meadows. Before she goes to sleep, Erika always makes a tiny glass out of birch bark and has a drink of blueberry juice mixed with honey from Eric's secret bees.

About the only thing Erika does not do with blueberries is brush her teeth with blueberry juice. That would give her blue teeth. So Erika uses Eric's magic beeswax and a tiny toothbrush made out of pine boughs instead.

Erika only eats meat once a year, on her birthday at a Chicago Cubs game when she meets her brother Alex (who has the same birthday) behind third base and eats one hot dog with mustard and sauerkraut during the seventh inning. One thing Erika never eats is eggs. To Erika, that would be like eating the children of her friends, the birds.

Whatever food Erika does not eat Erika puts back in her backpack. She always carries out of the wilderness whatever she carried in. She also picks up any litter she finds along the streams or trails. Erika hates litter and loves the woods as much as Eric. And just as Eric fixes skiing trails, so Erika fixes hiking trails. She makes sure they are well marked so that children and their families will not get lost. When Erika comes to a lean-to or a camping spot, she cleans it up with her broom made of pine boughs and leaves a big supply of blueberries. The woods and the streams are for everyone, thinks Erika, as long as we take care of them. And in a warming world full of cars, factories and buildings there is a lot Erika and everyone else need to do to take care of them.

Perhaps one day you will come to a lean-to that is so tidy, so clean, and so well-stocked with blueberries that you will think Erika had been there the night before. If the lean-to smells a little bit like beeswax and there is a blueberry patch nearby, you will probably be right. Then you will sleep with a smile on your face. And perhaps when you leave the

Eric the Skier

lean-to you will leave it as clean as Erika would. That would give Erika an even bigger smile. And she will sing like Papagena in her tiny birch bark canoe, surrounded by her friends, the birds, with her long blond hair spread out behind her like a banner on the wind.

James Kobak

Alex the Surfer, Eric's Younger Brother

Alex the surfer, Eric's younger brother, was born exactly one year after Eric and Erika. All three were born during the seventh inning stretch of a Chicago Cubs baseball game, but the game during which Alex was born took place a year after the game during which Eric and Erika were born so Eric and Erika have always been one year older than Alex. Try as hard as he might, swim as fast as he could, and hold his breath under water as long as he was able, Alex could never catch up. Eric, Erika, and Alex were all delivered by the same hot dog vendor. He later became a doctor. Eric sends him postcards, Erika sends him blueberries and Alex sends him cans of tuna fish.

When Alex was a baby, he cried and cried. That may be one reason Eric and Erika spent so much time outside the house. Come to think of it, that may be one reason their father did so much surveying and their mother went to so many meetings.

Alex only stopped crying when he was in the bathtub. Then Alex laughed and gurgled happily, as babies will do. The only other time Alex laughed was when a sudden rainstorm filled his baby carriage with water and got him soaking wet.

Alex's father took Alex on some of his surveying trips. But Alex did not like surveying ski resorts, as Eric did. Nor did Alex like surveying forests and jungles, as Erika did. He cried and cried and made it hard for his father to concentrate on his surveying. A lot of inaccurate maps resulted. Some of these can be seen in museums today. The only time Alex was happy was when his father was surveying an ocean or one of the Great Lakes. Unfortunately, surveying miles and miles of water bored Alex's father and tended to make him seasick.

Alex did not like to ski. He did not like to hike. He did not like to ride in a canoe. He only liked to be in the water. Alex was only happy when he was wet.

When he was five years old, Alex made a giant surfboard and two water skis from a redwood tree that Erika brought home for him from the forest. Now Alex surfs and water skis all over the world. When he is not surfing, he is usually snorkeling or scuba diving. When he is not doing that, Alex does the back float. Alex can float on his back for hours, days,

Eric the Skier

or even weeks. He is probably the best back floater who ever lived, even counting whales and dolphins.

Alex does not read nearly as much as Eric. Alex has started books like Moby Dick and The Old Man and the Sea several times, but could never finish them. The pages would get all wet, soggy, and blurry by the time he got to his favorite part, a description of the fish swimming. The same thing happened whenever he tried to read Aqua Man comic books.

Alex also does not sing nearly as much as Erika. Because of all his childhood crying, Alex has very strong lungs and could sing almost as loudly as Erika if he wanted. But whenever Alex opens his mouth wide to sing "We all live in a yellow submarine" or "Anchors Aweigh," water gets into it, interfering with his floating — to saying nothing of his singing. So Alex mostly hums to himself the Water Music of Handel or old Beach Boys songs as he swims.

The one thing Alex does love to do besides getting wet is painting. Alex only wears one type of clothing — bathing suits — but he owns hundreds and hundreds of them, different bathing suits for every day of the year, even for different hours of the day. Alex paints all these bathing suits himself. Sometimes he paints portraits of people on his bathing suits: famous swimmers like Johnny Weissmuller and Mark Spitz; or a self-portrait of himself floating; or even portraits of Eric on skis, Erika in her canoe, Edwina in her apartment, or his mother dancing or cooking, or his father surveying. Sometimes he paints portraits of fish or octopi or squid or jelly fish. Sometimes he paints seascapes or ships. Sometimes Alex paints squares; sometimes he paints circles. Alex might paint a triangle on one side of his bathing suit and a rectangle on the other; or polka dots on the front and diagonal lines on the back; or a series of tac-tac-toe games; or a scarlet A with flowers growing out of it; or a picture remembered from an Aqua Man comic book before the pages got so wet they all stuck together. Or sometimes Alex just draws designs with a lot of bright colors, or lets the paint drip on the bathing suit, or pours out the paint and spreads it around with his fingers. Then his bathing suit for that part of the day looks like the Aqua Man comic book after the pages got so wet that they all stuck together. Many of Alex's bathing suits are hanging in museums today.

Alex paints his bathing suits on a tiny island in the Caribbean. The island is not much bigger than Eric's cabin in the woods. It is far too small to be on any maps, not even any of the maps surveyed by his father. Only Erika and the fish who pose for the pictures on Alex's bathing suits know where the island is.

Color Island — for that would be the official name of the island if it were large enough to be on any map — has one large palm tree on it. Alex props his surfboard against the trunk and uses it for an easel. Then he sits under the palm tree and paints for exactly one hour. If it is hot, as it usually is, Alex may have a few drinks of coconut milk. Sometimes he mixes the coconut milk with the blueberries Erika sends him. On weekdays he drinks the mixture for energy; on weekends he uses it as paint.

Alex is such a good painter that he can paint while surfing or even when he is under water — except that then he has no easel. Alex can also paint while doing the back float, but then the paint drips all over him, and after a while it becomes impossible to tell what part of the painting is Alex's bathing suit and what part is Alex. So now Alex almost always paints his bathing suits under the palm tree. The paint dripping on the sand makes colorful patterns that look like oriental rugs. That is why, if the island were large enough to have a name, its name would be Color Island.

Alex is always suntanned, but never sunburned. Eric gives him a big tube of his special beeswax every Christmas, and Alex uses it every morning and afternoon as suntan lotion. The wax is also useful as shark repellent when Alex surfs through the South Pacific. If Alex runs out of beeswax, he uses blueberry and coconut milk and swims as fast as he can.

Alex eats only seafood. He particularly likes bluefish, rainbow trout, and red snapper: any colorful fish. They remind him of his bathing suits. Once or twice Alex has started to eat one of his colorful bathing suits by mistake.

Alex usually cooks his fish in a sauce of blueberries and coconut juice, with a pinch of beeswax to hide the fishy smell. If Alex is especially hungry, as he might be if he has water skied to Australia and back to go surfing, he makes a seafood ragout by adding seaweed and flotsam and jetsam. If the fish are not colorful enough, Alex throws in a little paint. Alex can actually cook a ragout while he is surfing. In fact Alex is one of the few people who can cook a ragout, paint a copy of Botticelli's Venus Rising from the Sea, rescue capsized sailors, and listen to "Little Deuce Coupe" on his portable radio, all at the same time and all while surfing through a typhoon on the Indian Ocean.

Alex sends seafood home to his mother and father and also gives a few fish to Eric and Erika whenever he sees them. His mother makes bouillabaisses and paellas out of the sea food Alex sends her. In other words, like all mothers, she can take anything and make it into stew. His father eats fish and seaweed sandwiches every day for a month after one of Eric's packages arrives. In other words, like all fathers, Alex's father can take anything and turn.it into sandwiches.

Erika loves to eat the fish Alex gives her while she is canoeing. So she is not just being polite when she says thank you very much for the delicious smoked electric eel. "I have never eaten anything else that lighted up when I put it in my mouth," says Erika.

Eric the skier always sends his brother a nice thank-you postcard for the fish. But unlike Erika, Eric really does not like them. As you know, fish remind Eric of water. And water reminds him of snow that has melted. And that makes Eric cry right into the middle of his tuna fish. So

Eric the Skier

Eric always leaves the fish Alex sends him for the hibernating bears and munches on his pepperoni and oatmeal cookies instead.

You would think the melting snow that makes so Eric sad would make Alex happy, since it means there would be more water. And most of the time it does. But sometimes there is too much melting snow, melting snow from warming weather. This much melting snow can make water too hot for the fish and coral reefs. Too much extra water can mean hurricanes, typhoons, and tides that might someday flood the woods and wash Color Island away. So when Alex swims near Alaska or Iceland and sees the glaciers he has been floating by and painting for years melting into the ocean or shrinking, he gets as sad as Eric. He floats on his back and paints these melting glaciers on his bathing suit in colors that are dark and drab compared to all his other paintings. He sends these bathing suits to museums to hang on their walls as a warning.

But this does not affect the new birthday card Alex paints on one of his bathing suits every year on his way to meet Erika behind third base at a Chicago Cubs baseball game. "Happy Birthday, Eric and Erika," it says in the front of the bathing suit in big, bright letters. "And happy birthday to me, too," it says on the back. Then, on her way to the baseball game, Erika sings "Happy Birthday" in her beautiful voice so loudly that it can be heard on top of a mountain thousands of miles away . If the mountain is high enough, Eric can see the birthday card, too. Then Eric smiles, dances a jig on his skis, and skis toward his secret cabin in the woods.

Sometime when you are swimming, listen carefully, especially if it is the day of a Chicago Cubs baseball game. Maybe you, too, will be able to hear Erika singing "Happy Birthday." Underwater, Erika's voice sounds like thousands of bells.

Or perhaps, if you climb a high mountain, or one with a fire tower, you will even see Alex's birthday card as a flash of bright color way off in the distance, at the edge of the horizon, where the sea meets the sky and the land disappears. For those are the closest things that exist to directions to Alex's home on Color Island.

Eric's Timid Sister, Edwina

Eric's sister Edwina was born on March 15 when, although he did not know it, Eric was fifteen years old. Eric happened to be home for a visit, skiing on the roof. He was reading Julius Caesar by William Shakespeare while practicing herringboning around the chimney. "Beware the Ides of March," read Eric in a loud voice. And just then Edwina was born.

As a baby, Edwina spent most of her time sleeping and eating. She did not cry, but she did not laugh or gurgle, either. Her father took Edwina surveying, but she never seemed happy. She just looked worried.

Her father said, "Oh, that's OK. Perhaps she just likes winter, like her brother, Eric." But winter came, and still Edwina did not look happy. She just looked cold and worried. Eric took Edwina skiing and gave her hours of skiing lessons without even asking for candy bars. But Edwina just looked colder and more worried.

"Oh, that's OK," said Edwina's mother. "She will probably like the spring and fall, like Erika." But spring came, and so did fall, and neither made Edwina happy. They just made her hot. Erika took Edwina on hikes through beautiful meadows. She put her in her tiny birch bark canoe and paddled past waterfalls and ponds full of swans. Erika even hummed the score of Swan Lake in her beautiful voice. But Edwina just got blisters and looked more worried than ever.

"Oh, that's OK," said Edwina's mother and father at the same moment. "Perhaps she just likes water, like her brother Alex." But beaches and swimming pools did not make Edwina happy, either. Alex took Edwina water skiing and surfing. He took her scuba diving through coral reefs filled with fish more colorful than any of his bathing suits. But Edwina just looked wet — wet and worried. She got sunburns and earaches and never could learn to do the back float.

The truth was that Edwina did not like to do any of these things. Everyone else in Edwina's family was always doing something — and usually they were doing several different things at the same time, like skiing and reading, or canoeing and singing, or cooking and aerobic dancing. But Edwina did not like to do anything.

Or rather I should say Edwina did one thing: worry. While everyone else in Edwina's family went everywhere and did everything, Edwina never went anywhere. But she worried about everything.

While Eric took her skiing, Edwina worried about skiing: What if I should fall down? Could I get back up? Would I have to see the doctor? Would he give me a shot? How much would it hurt? Would he give me a lollipop? What if I swallowed the lollipop stick? And that was just the beginning of Edwina's worrying. Eric could ski and ski for days. But Edwina could worry about skiing for even longer.

While Erika hiked and canoed, Edwina worried about hiking and canoeing: Will the pack be too heavy? What if I didn't take enough clothes? What if I brought too many clothes and can't stuff them all in the pack? What if a spider should get into the pack along with my extra clothes? Could it be a tarantula? How much do tarantula bites hurt? Would I have to go to the doctor? Will he give me a shot? Would he give me a lollipop? What if I swallowed the lollipop stick? And that was just the first five minutes of worrying. Erika hikes and canoes for days at a time. But Edwina can worry about hiking and canoeing for even longer.

While Alex surfed and scuba dived, Edwina worried about swimming: What if the water is polluted? What if it gives people rashes?

If I were to get a rash on top of sunburn, would I peel? If I peeled, would I attract sharks and poisonous jellyfish? How much does it hurt to be eaten by a shark and stung by a poisonous jelly fish? Would I have to go to the doctor? Will he give me a shot? Would he give me a lollipop? What if I swallowed the lollipop stick? And so on and so on as Edwina starts worrying about accidents and diseases that haven't even been discovered by doctors yet. If Alex finds a good tidal wave or tsunami in the Pacific Ocean, he can sometimes surf for a month. But Edwina can worry about surfing for even longer.

Edwina now lives in her own apartment with her pet cat, Worrywart. She tells some of her worries to Worrywart. But since Worrywart is a cat, it is hard to tell whether she pays much attention. Mostly, being a cat, Worrywart falls asleep and stretches and licks herself and falls asleep again and jumps up on the sofa and scratches the slip covers and falls asleep again. And all this time Edwina is worrying away. But it really doesn't matter much to Worrywart what Edwina is worrying about because every time Worrywart wakes up, Edwina has gotten her worrying around to doctors and shots and lollipop sticks again.

Edwina seems to do most of the worrying for Worrywart as well as for the rest of the family. Edwina does more than enough worrying for a whole zoo, let alone for one single cat. The only time Worrywart appears to worry for herself is when she finds no cat food in her crystal glass cat food dish.

Eric the Skier

Once a week Edwina goes to the supermarket to buy cat food for Worrywart and oatmeal for herself. Edwina's mother taught Edwina to cook all kinds of delicious foods when she was a child, but Edwina only eats oatmeal. She is too worried to eat any other kind of food. She might choke on it, or she might be allergic to it, or it might be too hot or too cold, or too sweet, or too sour, or too lumpy or too creamy, or too thick or too thin; or it might be too fattening or have too many carbohydrates or be proved at some later time to be harmful to someone who might turn out to be Edwina. So Edwina eats only oatmeal.

Eric and Erika send Edwina a package of delicious blueberries and honey from Eric's secret swarm of bees every March 15 for her birthday. Edwina sends them a thank-you postcard by carrier pigeon. But she never eats the blueberries or the honey. She is afraid she might choke on the blueberries or stain something with blueberry juice. She worries that the honey might have a bee stinger in it. How could she tell the doctor that she had swallowed a bee stinger by mistake if she were choking on a blueberry? And how embarrassed would she feel if she had to go to the doctor's office with a blueberry stain on her dress? So Edwina feeds the blueberries and honey to Worrywart.

Edwina's mother sends Edwina oatmeal cookies with raisins and nuts in them every month or so. Edwina sends a singing telegram that her mother can dance to say thank you. But Edwina never eats the oatmeal cookies. She is afraid she might swallow a raisin the wrong way or break a filling on a macadamia nut. Or she might leave some crumbs on the floor and the crumbs might attract ants which might turn out to be man-eating fire ants which might try to eat her and Worrywart. And that might mean that Edwina and Worrywart would have to go to the doctor and the vet, respectively. And that might mean shots and lollipops and lollipop sticks and all the rest. So Edwina picks out the raisins and nuts and feeds them to Worrywart. Then she grinds up the oatmeal cookies into oatmeal and eats it for dinner.

Edwina never leaves her apartment except to go to the supermarket. The supermarket is across the street, and it actually takes Edwina longer to get into and out of her apartment than it takes her to do the shopping. This is because Edwina has thirty-three locks of all different kinds and sizes on her apartment door: padlocks, safety locks, combination locks, bicycle locks, electronic locks, computerized locks and even rare antique locks from the time of the Spanish Inquisition. Edwina has all these locks because she is worried about, among other things, burglars and vandals and insurance salesmen and nosy neighbors and possible invading armies and aliens from outer space and escaped gorillas from the zoo. Of course, now that Edwina has all the locks, she worries constantly that she will forget the keys or the combinations, or that she might have forgotten to lock them all, or that all thirty-three locks will rust and fall off at the same time. So Edwina only goes out of the apartment once a week, to go shopping when Worrywart looks hungry.

Eric the Skier

Edwina reads for thirty-three minutes every day. She can't read for any longer than that because reading makes her nervous. If she reads a book she likes at the beginning, she worries that she won't keep on liking it until the end. Or she worries that she will like it so much that she will be sad when it is over. Or she worries that she will worry about all the characters in the book. If there is a character in the book who worries, Edwina worries about how much she will worry about what the character in the book is worrying about. This kind of complicated worrying gives even Edwina a headache.

Besides, Edwina worries that she might not finish a book before it is due at the library. Then she might have to pay a fine. She might forget to pay the fine and be arrested and have to go to prison. Then she might be in a jailbreak and be shot or hanged or given the electric chair and might forget to ask for oatmeal for her last meal. So to be sure that none of these things ever happens, and because worrying about her last meal has made her hungry, Edwina stops reading after thirty-three minutes and eats a big bowl of oatmeal instead.

Edwina does not often watch TV or listen to the radio. They worry her. She worries about what is on the news. Before she even hears the news, she worries about what might be on it. During the commercials before the news even begins Edwina can worry about six world wars, four revolutions, three giant volcanoes with mudslides and earthquakes, untold numbers of famines, plagues and pestilences, and knee injuries to every member of the New York football Giants. When game shows come on, Edwina worries about what the right answers are; when sports come on, she worries about the losing team; and when comedies come on, she worries about whether she will understand the jokes. Most of all she worries about how the TV or radio will remind her about the world getting warmer and how there may be more disasters for Erika to hike and paddle around, more storms and cyclones for Alex to surf or swim through, and less snow for Eric to ski on with his long yellow skis. So to avoid all these worries, and because worrying has made her hungry again, Edwina usually decides not to watch TV or listen to the radio any longer but to eat a second bowl of oatmeal instead.

You might think that music would relax Edwina and make her forget some of her worries. But alas, it isn't so. Edwina worries that if the music has too many loud low notes it will rattle all the oatmeal bowls in her cupboards; but if it has too many high notes, it might crack all the windows or Worrywart's crystal glass cat food dish. Edwina worries that she will never get the music just right.

And even if she did get the music just right, Edwina worries that she might want to sing along to the music and that singing along might give her a sore throat. Then she might have to go to the doctor who might give her a shot and then a lollipop for being so brave (though Edwina worries that she probably wouldn't be brave at all) and then she might swallow the lollipop stick. And how could she explain to the doctor that she had a lollipop stick stuck in her throat if she had laryngitis from singing too loud to music that was rattling her oatmeal bowls and cracking her only cat's only cat food dish?

And then Edwina worries that the neighbors might complain that she was singing too loudly and the police might come and Edwina might have to open the thirty-three locks on her apartment door to let in the police and then she would have to close up all thirty-three locks and she might miss one and Worrywart might run out of the apartment and meet a tomcat and have a litter of kittens and Edwina would have to take care of them. And what if she couldn't carry that much cat food home from the supermarket? In fact, Edwina can find enough to worry about for days in the Minute Waltz or even a simple song like "Twinkle, Twinkle, Little Star." So to avoid these problems, and because thinking, about cat food has made her hungry yet again, Edwina decides not to sing or hum or put on a record, but to eat a third bowl of oatmeal instead.

Since Edwina worries so much, and worrying makes her so hungry, Edwina eats a lot of oatmeal. About as many oats go into her oatmeal as are eaten by a stable of champion racehorses on the morning of the Kentucky Derby. Edwina worries so much about eating oatmeal from used bowls because of the germs that they might have that she has hundreds and hundreds of oatmeal bowls and dozens of cupboards in which to put them.

Edwina has almost as many oatmeal bowls as Alex has bathing suits. In fact, Alex painted all of Edwina's oatmeal bowls so that they would look like his bathing suits.

The oatmeal bowls are the only colorful things in Edwina's apartment. All the furniture is gray; all the curtains are gray; all of Edwina's clothes are gray. Even Worrywart the cat is gray, except for his whiskers, which are grayish white. Edwina herself is gray because she never goes outside. And as you have probably already guessed, Edwina's hair is gray from worrying so much. All of Edwina's hair had turned gray by her third birthday because by then she had already worried more than people who are eighty or ninety years old worry in their entire lives.

The cupboards for the oatmeal bowls take up most of the space in Edwina's apartment. The only other furniture in the apartment is a small bureau full of Edwina's gray clothes; a small gray sofa on which a large gray cat (Worrywart) is usually curled; a bed with a large gray comforter on it; a stove with a pot full of gray oatmeal cooking on it; a small table with a gray tablecloth for eating oatmeal on; a gray refrigerator full of gray oatmeal; and a gray umbrella stand full of gray umbrellas. (Even though Edwina almost never goes outside, she has lots of umbrellas because she always worries about the weather.)

Of course Edwina does not really need any more furniture since she never gives parties or has any visitors. The idea of visitors terrifies Edwina because of all the extra things to worry about: Where to put the

Eric the Skier

coats? Where to put the visitors? What to say? What to do? Will the visitors like oatmeal? If not, will they like cat food? What if one of the visitors is a doctor with a lollipop with a stick that Edwina might swallow? So Edwina almost never has any visitors except her sister Erika, who sweeps the apartment once a year with her broom made out of pine boughs; her brother Alex, who scrubs the sinks and fixes the plumbing; and her brother Eric, who cleans out the inside of the refrigerator with baking soda that looks just like snow and a spoonful of his magic honey.

Edwina's mother and father did come to visit one Thanksgiving Day, right after Edwina first moved into the apartment. Her father wanted to survey the apartment, and her mother wanted to cook Eggs Benedict on the stove. But early in the morning Edwina began to worry about what might happen if the eggs her mother wanted to cook should suddenly hatch and turn into chickens and be eaten by Worrywart who might leave feathers all over the apartment. That might make Edwina sneeze and sneeze until she had to go to the doctor who might give her a lollipop with a stick — a stick that she might swallow in the middle of a sneeze. So Edwina just left two bowls of oatmeal on the gray table and spent the afternoon hiding in bed under her gray comforter.

Because she worries so much about visitors, Edwina hates holidays. At Christmas time she worries that carolers might knock on her door unexpectedly or that Santa Claus might drop in and Edwina would have to worry about whether he would get stuck in the chimney. On

Halloween there are all those trick-or-treaters. Most people know that the trick-or-treaters are not really Batman and Aqua Man, or bandits and pirates, or Darth Vader, or ghosts or skeletons or witches. Most people know they are children. Even Edwina knows that. But since she worries every day that all those monsters and villains will actually come to her apartment, Edwina cannot help worrying that the little six-year-old in a Darth Vader mask might really be Darth Vader or that the second-grader with a bandana over her face really is Billy the Kid or Jessie James or some other notorious bandit. And even if Edwina did not worry about that, all the children who come to her apartment door dressed as horrid bad men or frightening creatures just remind her of all the things she will have to worry about the rest of the year.

Even on Valentine's Day Edwina worries that the postman might come by to deliver cards and letters. Edwina worries about having to open and close all the thirty-three locks on her apartment door. And what if the postman should frighten Worrywart, who might knock over the oatmeal on the stove or frighten Edwina, who might bump into the cupboards and lose all her keys and have a concussion and get a bruise on her knee and have to go to the doctor? And you know what might happen then! That's right. Edwina might get a shot and a lollipop and swallow the stick and not even know it!

Edwina worries so much that, when not eating oatmeal or shopping once a week, she spends most of her time in bed curled up in her gray comforter. Edwina's comforter weighs 115 pounds. This is exactly as much as Edwina and Worrywart weigh after Edwina has had several bowls of oatmeal and Worrywart has had a crystal glass bowl full of cat food. It is also exactly the weight of Eric's yellow skis, Erika's largest birch bark canoe, and all the paint that Alex spills in one year of painting.

Sometimes Edwina gets up from her bed and looks out the window. But then she looks at the sky and begins to worry that there might be a tornado or hurricane or that Halley's Comet might return unexpectedly forty-nine years early and hit her apartment building, destroying all her oatmeal dishes. Then Edwina looks at the supermarket and the other buildings across the street. But this just makes Edwina begin to worry even more — about all the things that all the people in the buildings might be worrying about. Finally, Edwina looks down to the street. And then she begins to worry in earnest: about street crime and litter and traffic accidents. She worries about noise pollution, gridlock, and jaywalking. She worries about parking tickets. She worries about how scary it would be to drive a big car or a small car or a big truck or a small truck or a van or a motorcycle or even a tricycle or skateboard. Most of all, she worries about pollution and climate change. Edwina gets so worried that she pulls down the window shade, checks to make sure that all the thirty-three locks on her apartment door are locked, sits down at her table with the gray tablecloth, and eats a big bowl of oatmeal. Then Edwina pats Worrywart three times and climbs into her bed. Edwina wraps the gray comforter tightly around her and worries herself to sleep.

One thing that happens right outside Edwina's window every year is the Fourth of July parade. This causes Edwina no end of worry. She worries about the noise, of course. And of course she worries about the crowds and the litter. But she worries about other things, too: what if the bagpipers run out of breath? What if the mayor forgets to wave and doesn't get any votes in the next election? What if all the Cub Scouts and Brownies have tired feet and blisters, as Edwina always had as a child whenever she went hiking with her sister, Erika? What if one of the drums breaks or the fifes are filled with chewing gum or a drum majorette throws her baton high in the air and the law of gravity is suddenly suspended and it never comes back down? What if some of the soldiers start marching the wrong way and knock down the American Legion, the Elks Club, and the high school band?

So now, whenever it is the Fourth of July, Edwina wakes up early in the morning and makes sure the window shade is all the way down. She makes sure all the thirty-three locks on her door are secure and that the cat food is heaped high in Worrywart's crystal glass cat food dish. Edwina eats two large bowls of oatmeal because she knows how upset she is going to be. Then, before the parade begins, Edwina puts ear plugs in her ears, gets into her bed and pulls her gray comforter tightly around her. And there she sits all day in the dark and the silence as outside the parade goes on and the bands play and the mayor and the governor and even the water commissioner wave at the crowd and the soldiers march and the sun shines and the people eat hot dogs and cheer the bagpipers and the fifes and the drum majorettes.

While Eric skis down Mt. Everest with the sun on his face, there sits Edwina in her darkened gray room. While Erika hikes through wildflowers in Switzerland, singing and surrounded by birds, Edwina sits in her little gray bed, wrapped in her heavy gray comforter. And there Edwina sits, staring at her sleeping gray cat, while Alex scuba dives among the tiger fish or surfs in the sunlight with leaping dolphins.

James Kobak

Eric The Skier Falls In Love

    One year Erika paddled Eric across the Atlantic Ocean for some late spring skiing in the United States. Alex water-skied behind the canoe in some of his brightest, most fluorescent bathing suits.

    The changing climate made it a stormy voyage. Alex tried surfing and then water-skiing but at last had to hang on for dear life while doing the back float all the way from Calais to Bermuda. Erika's friends, the birds, were tossed by furious winds, and many turned back at the Canary Islands. Huge waves cascaded into the canoe. Eric and Erika had to bail out the canoe with their backpacks, melting most of Eric's snow. Eric was wet one day and seasick the next and even more miserable than he usually was when surrounded by water. Erika and the few brave sea gulls flying through the storms sang "Raindrops Keep Falling on My Head" and "Singing in the Rain." Eric moaned along a little out of tune in the bottom of the canoe.

Because of the storms, it took a long time for the canoe to reach the United States. Erika paddled through March, through April, through May. June came and went, and still Erika was paddling. Alex was still doing the back float and hanging on for dear life. And Eric was still moaning in the bottom of the canoe.

Finally, when Erika did not think she could paddle another stroke, and Eric did not think he could moan another moan, the sun came out. And just then the birch bark canoe (along with Alex, right next to it) floated into New York harbor.

The harbor was beautiful. Boats were everywhere: sail boats and yachts and ocean liners and tugboats; big boats and little boats, and old boats and new boats. The boats were all different colors, and flags and pennants were flying from every mast. The harbor was as colorful as it could be — not as colorful as one of Alex's bathing suits of course, but as colorful as anything else could be.

Many of the flags were American flags. Alex looked at his waterproof wristwatch, which could tell the time, date and when it would be high tide in any of one hundred countries: today was the Fourth of July.

Eric the Skier

"Hurray," shouted Alex and immediately changed (underwater, of course) into a bathing suit he had painted red, white, and blue.

"Hurray," shouted Erika as hundreds of pigeons flocked to her canoe. And Erika started to sing "Yankee Doodle Dandy" in her beautiful voice, a voice that made the people on their boats stop talking and listen in the middle of their cocktail parties.

"Hurray," shouted Eric. "If there were any snow, it would be a fin day for skiing." Eric began reciting the Declaration of Independence. He recited it beautifully, even if he did pronounce "life, liberty and pursuit of happiness" as "lif, liberty and pursuit of snow," and even if he did think that "lif" referred to a ski lift and the Declaration of Independence was about skiing.

"We must call our sister Edwina," Erika said suddenly. "She is always so sad on the Fourth of July." So Eric, Erika, and Alex paddled to shore to find a phone, since their cell phones were all soaking wet and not working (as well as covered with seaweed). The first person they saw was the mayor, who was giving a speech. The mayor was glad to see Eric, Erika, and Alex, especially as it was an election year. He was so glad that he stopped his speech, pinned medals on them and let Erika use his phone, The audience was glad to see Eric, Erika, and Alex, too, because it meant that they might not have to hear the end of the mayor's speech.

Erika punched in Edwina's number. The phone rang and rang, and then it rang some more. But of course Edwina would not answer it until it rang thirty-three times. Edwina never answered her phone until it rang thirty-three times because only her family would let a phone ring that many times without hanging up.

Edwina never answered the phone before it rang thirty-three times on the Fourth of July or any other day. She was too worried to answer it. It might be the President of the United States calling to tell Edwina she would be the next ambassador to France. And that would mean new clothes and strange foods and passports and airplane tickets and all kinds of complications, including shots. And you know what that means: lollipops with sticks capable of being swallowed. And how would Edwina ever tell the doctor she had swallowed a lollipop stick when she did not know the French word for lollipop, lollipop stick or even swallow?

So while the phone rang and rang, Edwina sat and sat, huddled on her gray bed eating oatmeal under her gray comforter with the gray window shades pulled all the way down and her large gray cat Worrywart (who had just gotten up after sleeping through the first thirty two rings) eating cat food from a crystal glass cat food bowl in the middle of her gray apartment.

It takes a long time for a telephone to ring thirty-three times, and after the thirty-second ring the mayor did decide to make another speech, even if it was a short speech, especially for the mayor. By then the sun was setting, and it was too late to call Edwina, who would be falling asleep under her gray comforter. So Alex, Eric, and Erika returned to Erika's birch bark canoe and had dinner. They ate stewed blueberry tarts covered with whipped cream and seafood sauce. This dinner was red, white, and blue for the Fourth of July and was also the only food all three of them could agree upon.

As they ate, the sky began to darken, almost as if it were the planetarium to which their father used to take them as children while he practiced surveying in the dark. A star appeared. Erika wished for gentle winds for her friends, the birds. Alex wished for new paint and new bathing suits on which to splash it. And of course Eric wished for snow. That was what he always wished for, even in July.

A tremendous explosion soon put an end to wishing. Then came another and another, each louder than the one before, each even louder than Erika could sing. Suddenly the night sky was ablaze with light. Flares and rockets filled the darkness, tracing colorful patterns over the ships and buildings. For tonight was the Fourth of July fireworks. On and on the fireworks went, cascades of light tumbling through the darkness: bursts of yellow and orange petals and floating little flakes of green.

The sky looked as if one of Alex's bathing suits had come to life. In fact Alex began to talk excitedly about the designs he could make with fireworks if only he had a bathing suit large enough and he did not have to wear it while the fireworks were exploding.

As Alex floated on his back into the middle of the harbor to get a better view, an amber flash burst over the Statute of Liberty and caught Eric's eye. Eric had never seen anything so beautiful. And he was not looking at the fireworks like Alex. No, Eric was looking at the Statue of Liberty herself.

Eric had never seen a woman so strong or so noble. He had never seen anyone with such a look of conviction on her face. He had never seen anyone who looked as if she could manage Eric's three hundred fifteen centimeter skis.

Eric was stunned. Without realizing it, he stood up in the canoe — a foolish thing to do at any time. Without realizing what he was doing, Eric dove out of the canoe and swam across the harbor like a moth to a flame. This was an even more foolish thing to do because moths cannot swim. And neither could Eric. But fortunately Eric's long yellow skis kept him afloat until Alex swam by to rescue him.

Alex dragged Eric ashore on Liberty Island, right at the feet of the Statue of Liberty. As soon as he saw that Eric was wet but otherwise all right, Alex left him and back floated out to sea. Alex wanted to get back to Color Island to start painting new bathing suit designs.

Eric was wet, all right. He had seaweed in his goggles, water in his ski boots, and jellyfish bobbing in his backpack. Eric was as wet as wet can be. But Eric never noticed. He just sat on Liberty Island with his long yellow skis, looking up at the Statue of Liberty's brave face as

Eric the Skier

fireworks exploded all around it. "I love you," said Eric. "You are very beautiful," said Eric. "You are a fin-looking statue," he said.

Eric recited Romeo's speeches from Romeo and Juliet and Marc Anthony's speeches from Anthony and Cleopatra. He recited poems of love in many languages. Eric was very excited and recited faster and faster, waving his ski poles for emphasis. The poems and the languages started getting all jumbled up together, and the fireworks kept exploding in the middle of Eric's sonnets and villanelles. So when Eric meant to say,

"Come live with me and be my love,"

it sounded like,

"Come blam blam blam and boom boom boom."

Of course some of the poetry Eric recited sounded like that even when there were no fireworks.

Eric recited and recited, but the Statue of Liberty was silent. A few times her lips seemed to curl up slightly into a smile; once or twice a few tears almost seemed to trickle down her large metal cheeks. It could have been only flashes of light from the fireworks that made it seem as if the Statue of Liberty were smiling and crying. Perhaps it was Eric's ski poles that made the Statue smile and cry — if that is what the Statue really did. After all, the poles may have tickled her feet just a little when Eric waved them about at the base of the statue. Or perhaps — just perhaps — the Statue was as much in love with Eric as Eric was with the Statue.

Eventually the fireworks ended. The mayor shook hands and went to bed. The big boats sailed away. So did the little boats. The tugboats towed the last ocean liner out to sea. At last even Erika paddled away, up the Hudson River, toward the Catskills and the Adirondacks, in her birch bark canoe.

"Goodbye, Eric," said Erika as she paddled upstream, followed by hundreds of sea gulls and pigeons. But Eric never answered her. Eric just stared up at the Statue of Liberty.

The clock struck midnight. Even in New York City all was quiet. All those buildings, and not a light shone anywhere. Not a subway moved in that great city; not a taxi honked. Not an alley cat purred; not a policeman blew his whistle.

Then Eric heard the Statue of Liberty's voice. Or thought he did, for no one will ever know if the Statue of Liberty actually spoke to Eric, or if Eric only dreamed it. Even Eric will never know for sure.

The voice that Eric heard, or thought he heard, was the most beautiful Eric had ever heard, even more beautiful than his mother's singing in the kitchen or Erika's singing Mozart on the Danube in her birch bark canoe. The voice sounded like the tinkling of hundreds of church bells. It seemed to float on the air above him and then fall gently to his ears, like little flakes of powder snow falling on the slopes of Aspen.

Eric the Skier

"Oh, Eric, I am only a statue," the beautiful voice said. Or so it seemed to Eric. "I cannot go off and ski with you. Not even you could teach a big, old, heavy statue like me to ski."

"But I have taught children and pets and even big, old, heavy lawyers that looked like statues to ski," said Eric.

"Oh, I love you, Eric," said the voice of tinkling bells. "But I love everyone who wants to be free, whether it is to ski or to write poems or simply to sit in a room, like your sister Edwina. That is why I must always stand here for everyone to see — in the rain, in the snow, in the heat of the summer and the cold of winter. Everyone has their own idea of freedom. It is your idea of freedom that you love in me. You only love me the most because you are most free."

Eric began to realize that what the statue said, or seemed to say, was true. "Goodbye," he said. "You are as beautiful as moonlit snow," he said. "I will never forget you," he said.

"Goodbye, Eric," said the Statue of Liberty. Or so it seemed to Eric. And then it seemed to Eric that just for an instant the great stone statue bent down as if she were a schoolgirl picking up a fallen leaf and kissed his cheek. And, just for an instant, it seemed as if the cheeks of that stone statue blushed the color of a brand new penny, and her torch burned a deep, bright orange. To Eric the kiss felt like a snowflake and the torch looked like the winter sun.

Eric slowly got up on his long yellow skis. Slowly he started to ski toward Grand Central Station in the middle of New York. Eric was going to ski behind train after train until he reached the snow-covered mountains of Alaska.

"Goodbye, Eric," said the voice of the Statue. "I belong right here," said the Statue. "But it is a fin day for skiing somewhere else."

"I don't want to upset anyone," called Eric to the statute. "I just want to ski."

Eric never did forget the Statue of Liberty and the shy smile he thought he had seen in the glow of the orange sunbursts and green streamers that exploded all around her that warm July night. Eric tacked a postcard of the Statue of Liberty onto the wall of his secret cabin in the woods. He found a small plastic souvenir pencil sharpener in the shape of the Statue of Liberty on the sidewalk and put it in his backpack, right next to his mother's oatmeal cookies. Eric sometimes took the statue out and looked at it when he was lonely, which he sometimes found he was, even in the middle of a game of freeze tag with the deer. Once or twice when he was hungry, he almost took a bite out of the statue by mistake.

Sometimes, too, Eric would stop in the middle of skiing and gaze off into the distance in the direction of New York City. And sometimes then the Statue of Liberty's torch would seem to burn a little more brightly, and just for a moment a shy smile would seem to steal across her face. But people would say it was only the shadow of a passing cloud.

Eric the Skier

And sometimes at midnight on the Fourth of July, the Statue of Liberty may turn her head, just for an instant, toward Eric's cabin in the woods. Then her lips may open and form words. And although no one ever hears them, the words they form are "Eric" and "I love you" and "I hope tomorrow is a fin day for skiing wherever you are."

Now it may be only a coincidence, but wherever Eric is on the fifth of July — and he could be almost anywhere —- it is always an especially fine day for skiing. In fact, the first thing Eric always says on the fifth of July is, "It's a fin day for skiing." But of course that is the first thing Eric says every day. In fact, it is what he says most of the time. That, and the last words he spoke to the Statue of Liberty: "I don't want to upset anyone. I just want to ski."

James Kobak

Eric the Skier at the North Pole

One cold December evening Eric went off for a moonlight ski. It was a beautiful night; the moon hung in the sky like a great orange basketball. Except to Eric, it did not look like a basketball. Eric had never seen a basketball. Eric was always skiing outside when people were playing basketball indoors. To Eric, it looked like a giant earmuff or one of the Os in a tic-tac-toe game painted on a bathing suit by his brother, Alex.

It was such a beautiful night that Eric skied for hours and hours, reciting the poem, "'Twas the night before Christmas." Eric bent down low and skied under pine branches while he whispered, "Not a creature was stirring, not even a mouse." Then he started skiing faster as he said, "Raced to the window and threw open the sash." And he put himself into his fastest racing tuck and stabbed his poles into the frozen tundra for extra speed as he shouted, "On Dancer, on Prancer, on Donner and Vixen!" Eric almost reached disaster when he reached, "To the top of the rooftop, to the top of the wall, Now dash away, dash away, dash away all!," as he was face to face with Mount McKinley at the time, but Eric did a tremendous trick somersault he had practiced while skiing off his roof as a little boy and skied to the end of the poem as easily as most people walk to the bus stop.

    Since Eric could cover hundreds of miles in an hour when he was skiing his fastest, and since there had been many lines in the poem about flying reindeer requiring especially fast skiing, Eric soon entered the Arctic Circle. He skied on over the ice floes, slaloming between igloos and the deer and polar bears, who were barking greetings to the sea lions who swam along under the ice. Eric had conversations with many penguins who asked to be remembered to his sister, Erika. Eric tried to teach some of the penguins how to ski, but the backs of their skies kept getting crossed because of the funny way they walk, and they kept falling in the water. Even Eric found it difficult to ski the way penguins walk. But of course Eric never fell in the water because Eric hates water. Water reminds Eric of melted snow, which makes him so sad that he can scarcely bear to take a bath or shower in it, let alone fall in it with his skis on.

Eric the Skier

Eric started to recite the "Night Before Christmas" again. As soon as he got to "What to my wondering eyes should appear," something red appeared, due north far off in the distance. The red thing quickly got bigger and bigger because of the speed at which Eric was skiing.

"Ho, ho, ho," said the red thing suddenly.

"It's a fin day for skiing," said Eric.

"Happy Christmas to all, and to all a good night," said the red thing, which Eric could now see had black boots and a long white beard.

"I don't want to upset anyone; I just want to ski," said Eric.

"And what would you like for Christmas?" said the red thing. Eric could now see that the red thing had a smiling face with a pipe in it. The red thing also had a shoulder with a big brown sack slung over it.

"It's a fin day for skiing," said Eric.

"Ho, ho, ho," said the red thing, which Eric could now see was rather short and a good deal overweight like some of the lawyers to whom Eric sometimes gave skiing lessons. Eric also noted that the figure smelled faintly of reindeer.

The conversation went back and forth like this for some time, with many a "ho, ho, ho" and "Fin day for skiing" and "Happy Christmas to all" and Eric not wanting to upset anyone. Eric had a feeling that the red figure seemed familiar, but he could not quite place him. The red figure also seemed uncertain as to who Eric might be and kept forgetting about Eric's long yellow skis. He had to keep darting out of the way every time Eric moved to observe from a slightly different vantage point that it was a fin day for skiing.

Finally, Eric said, "Why, you must be Santa Claus. You brought me my first pair of skis."

And then Santa Claus — for that is indeed who it was, as you probably figured out long before Eric, who has never been too quick to get to the point about anything, unless he can find some way to relate it to skiing — said, "And you must be Eric. I had a devil of a time getting those long skis down your chimney. And aren't you some relation to that person Edwina with the thirty-three locks on her door and barbed wire on her chimneys who always wants oatmeal for Christmas?"

After that Santa and Eric went back to Santa Claus's house and had a long chat about what the snow is like on Christmas Eve. Eric met Santa's wife, who was aerobic dancing with some of the elves. They all drank lots and lots of cocoa. For Eric, it was almost like being back home, except that outside there were miles and miles of fresh, unused snow, stretching as far as the eye could see.

During the course of their chat, Eric told Santa that he had always wondered what it was like to drive a sleigh of flying reindeer. It sounded almost as much fun as ski jumping. And Santa told Eric that he had not been skiing for many years. Now Santa and Eric are both very polite. So

Eric the Skier

of course Eric offered to let Santa use his long yellow skis, even though they had never been on anyone else's feet. And of course Santa offered to let Eric use his sleigh and his reindeer, even though they had never before been driven by anyone else.

"It's a fin day for skiing," said Eric as he helped Santa on with the skis and reminded him of how to snowplow.

"Thank you, ho, ho, ho," said Santa.

"Happy Christmas to all," said Santa as he handed Eric the reins to the sleigh and told him secret commands used to control the reindeer and showed him the secret brake in the bottom of the sleigh.

"Zankyou," said Eric. I don't want to upset anyone; I just want to sleigh."

Off Eric went in Santa's sleigh, pulled by Santa's reindeer, off toward Canada and up toward the moon. Off went Santa on Eric's long yellow skis, out the front door and into the snow and the deep, dark woods.

Higher and higher went Eric, and farther and farther away. Soon he decided that he had gone high enough and far enough. In fact, Eric actually thought he might already have gone a bit too high and too far. That's all right, thought Eric to himself, I will snowplow. But Eric forgot he was not on his skis. He snowplowed with his feet, and nothing happened.

That's all right, thought Eric to himself, I will use the secret command. Unfortunately, the commands were secret all right, so secret that Eric had already forgotten them.

That's all right, thought Eric to himself, I will use the secret hand brake in the bottom of the sleigh. But the brake was secret all right, so secret that Eric could not find it. Every time he pulled what he thought was the brake he found he was holding the leg of a Barbie doll or a baseball bat or a cheerleader's baton.

Eric started shouting all the words he knew in the hopes that some of them might be the secret commands. He shouted "mogul" and "telemark" and "lift ticket." He shouted "parallel" and "kick turn" and "Jean Claude Killy." But what he shouted the most were "Help" and "SOS" and "I don't want to upset anyone; I just want to ski."

Some of the words Eric shouted must have been the secret commands because the sleigh swooped to the left and swooped to the right. It turned loop-the-loops and figure eights. It was very beautiful to see — but not to be inside. Before Eric knew what had happened, he found himself soaking wet. For Eric had caused Santa Claus's Christmas sleigh and all the reindeer to plunge right into the Atlantic Ocean.

Eric was very sad, sitting in all that water, seeing nothing but melted snow everywhere he looked. Also very frightened because Eric could not swim, and neither could the reindeer. Fortunately for Eric — and for every child who gets presents from Santa's sleigh — the sea lions

Eric the Skier

and penguins in the Arctic Circle had seen what was happening. The penguins told some sea gulls, who swooped into the United States to tell some robins who flew to tell Eric's sister Erika. The sea lions dove underwater and told some passing narwhals, who swam to tell Eric's brother Alex as he was basking under the sun on Color Island. Alex quickly swam back with the narwhals and ferried all the reindeer to safety, even Vixen who was a constant complainer. Erika paddled Eric to shore in her birch bark canoe, towing the sleigh and singing, "I'm dreaming of a white Christmas" and "Let it snow, let it snow," which she knew were two of Eric's favorite Christmas songs.

Alex was a little chilly up in the North Pole, dressed as he was in only a bathing suit (though quite a colorful one), so he said goodbye as soon as everyone — and every reindeer — was safely ashore. Alex swam back to Color Island to paint a picture of Santa's sleigh plunging into the ocean on one of his bathing suits. (It is hanging in a museum today.). The narwhals left, too, quite sadly. They had become good friends with the reindeer on the trip. That is one reason narwhals have horns: it reminds them of antlers.

Finally, after being introduced to about a thousand penguins and making sure that Eric would write a postcard to his sister Edwina telling her that he was perfectly safe, Erika left, singing "Michael Row the Boat Ashore" in her beautiful voice that sounded like thousands of bells. Erika actually could remember the name of every one of the penguins to whom she had been introduced. But penguins look so much alike that she always had trouble telling which penguin went with which name.

Eric could not ski back to Santa Claus's house because Santa Claus was wearing his skis. So he hitched the reindeer up to the sleigh and drove slowly back, making sure to do his driving on the ice, not the air. Vixen complained bitterly about having to walk rather than fly first class with The Big Claus himself, as she put it, but the other reindeer were glad just to be out of the water. They knew the way back by heart so Eric had nothing to do but sit in the sleigh. Or I should say sit in the sleigh and worry, because Eric was sure that he had wrecked Santa's sleigh by getting it all wet and rusty. Eric worried that he might even have wrecked Christmas. Eric worried so hard he almost thought he was Edwina.

Meanwhile, Santa had tried to use Eric's skis. Now once upon a time Santa, as a young elf, had been a very good skier. But Santa had not done much skiing in many years, and he was a good deal heavier than he had been as a young elf. Santa had also never skied on any skis nearly as long or as slippery as Eric's long yellow skis. No one but Eric had ever done that. No one but Eric could do that.

As soon as Santa skied out the front door and turned back to tell Mrs. Claus, "Look at how well I am skiing," he realized he could not control the skis. Because he could not control the skis he could not stop, and he could not turn around to get back to the house. Santa had as much trouble controlling Eric's skis as Eric had controlling Santa's sleigh.

Luckily for Santa, there was no Atlantic Ocean nearby to plunge into. But not so luckily for him, there were many rocks and trees. Soon Santa no longer looked like a red thing off in the distance. He looked like a red and black and blue thing. Even Santa's famous red suit was black and blue that Christmas.

Santa found himself heading straight for a huge redwood tree. He tried to remember to snowplow as Eric had taught him. But the way Eric had done it looked very easy. This seemed very hard. "Ho, ho, ho," said Santa as he covered his eyes. But it wasn't a very emphatic "Ho, ho, ho." "Clunk," said the rest of Santa Claus as he crashed straight into the tree. It was a very emphatic "Clunk."

Santa's stomach prevented him from being seriously hurt. It actually made him bounce off the big redwood tree onto smaller pine and spruce trees until at last he came to rest against a tiny tamarack. Santa felt a little like the pinball in the games he sometimes delivered at Christmas. But then Santa looked down to see if Eric's skis were still all right. And then Santa felt much worse.

For Eric's skis were not all right at all. One of them, the left one, had a big crack in it all along the tip, and the other, the right, had a jagged hole on the tail. In a few minutes Santa had done what had never happened in years and years of skiing. Santa had ruined Eric's pair of skis.

Slowly Santa sat down and took the skis off. Slowly he put them over his shoulder and trudged back through the snow toward his house. Santa did not say "Ho, ho, ho" or "Happy Christmas to all and to all a good night" or anything at all. For the first time in history, there was no smile on Santa's face.

Eric and Santa arrived back at Santa's house at almost the same moment. "I have something terrible to tell you," each started to say to the other at exactly the same time. "Oh, excuse me, I didn't mean to interrupt," each said at the same time. "No, you go first," each started to say to the other at exactly the same time. "Santa, I've ruined your sleigh," said Eric. And "Eric, I've ruined your skis," said Santa. But since they both said these things at the same time, neither could understand what the other was saying.

Having heard so much conversation outside, which was rather unusual for the North Pole, Mrs. Claus opened the door. She made both Santa and Eric come inside. She made Eric change out of his wet clothes and Santa put band-aids on some of his cuts. Then she had them both sit down and take turns speaking.

Eric, being the guest, went first. "Oh, Santa, I'm terribly sorry, but I forgot all the secret commands, and I made your sleigh fall into the water, and now it's all rusted and ruined and you won't be able to use it to bring any gifts to children, not even the poorest children."

Eric the Skier

Santa still did not look happy. But it was not because of anything that Eric had told him. It was only because of Eric's skis. "Why, Eric, that's nothing to worry about," said Santa. "My sleigh gets rusty every year from flying around through the snow and the morning dew when I'm on my way back to the North Pole. All it needs is a little wax."

"Wax? Why didn't you say so?" said Eric and took some of his magic beeswax out of his backpack. The wax came from the secret hive of magic bees in a secret meadow that only Eric and his sister Edwina have ever seen.

Santa gave the wax to Vixen to clean up the sleigh because she had been very unpleasant and had not helped with the dishes for several weeks. Vixen complained about what all that waxing would do to her hooves and many other things, of course, but she did a beautiful job of waxing because she was a very capable reindeer. Soon the sleigh looked good as new. It smelled even better than new. Even Vixen could not complain about that. Eric left some magic beeswax with the Clauses as a thank-you present. They used it to get some of the reindeer smell out of the house, and on special occasions Mrs. Claus even used it as eau de cologne.

Now it was Santa's turn to tell Eric what had happened to his skis, "Eric, my sleigh is as good as new, but I am afraid I cannot say the same about your skis." And slowly Santa went outside and got them, laid them on the floor, and showed Eric the long crack on the left tip and the jagged hole on the right tail.

Eric, who was in a very good mood by now, started to laugh. He almost started to say, "Ho, ho, ho" but did not think that appropriate in Santa Claus's own home.

"Santa, there is no problem at all," said Eric, and he took out some more magic beeswax from his great green backpack. "Wax, why didn't you say so?" laughed Eric and started to spread it over the crack in the tip and the hole in the tail. For Eric often got cracks and holes and nicks in his ski poles from skiing so hard and so fast, but he could always fix them just like new by heating his magic beeswax to just the right temperature. And so it was with his long yellow skis on this cold December evening.

Only, inside Santa Claus's house it did not seem cold anymore. It seemed as warm as July or August. And it had all the warmth of piping hot cocoa, to which Eric and Santa and even Mrs. Claus helped themselves often to celebrate their good fortune.

At last it was daybreak. Santa had to work on his toys, especially his toys for poor children. "Give them all skis," suggested Eric, but Santa gave them things they wanted more, things that only Santa knew about. Eric had to go, too — not to work, of course, but to ski.

"Goodbye, Mr. and Mrs. Claus," said Eric. "Zankyou for a very nice time."

"Goodbye, Eric," said Mr. and Mrs. Claus.

"Thank you for visiting and letting me use your skis," said Santa. "But don't ever let me use them again."

"I won't," said Eric. "And don't you ever let me use your sleigh again."

"Happy Christmas to all, and to all a good night," said Santa.

"It's a fin day for skiing," said Eric.

"Ho, ho, ho," said Santa.

In fact, Eric and Santa said these things back and forth several times. But finally Eric put his brown poles on the snow and pushed away from Santa's doorstep.

"I don't want to upset anyone; I just want to ski," called Eric behind him as he skied away across the Arctic icebergs. "And I mean ski, not sleigh," said Eric to himself as he skied toward distant forests with his long yellow skis gleaming like new and his backpack brimming with brand new snow from the very top of the world.

James Kobak

Eric the Skier and the St. Louis Arch

Eric began to notice a few years ago that every spring the warm days seemed to come a little sooner and to be a little warmer, melting the snow in some places where he used to be able to ski for an entire day. On one such warm spring day Eric the Skier found himself in the middle of the Mississippi River. This was a very bad place for Eric to find himself because Eric could not swim. In fact, Eric hated water because it reminded him of melted snow, something so unbearably sad that Eric hated even to think about it.

Eric had started out spring skiing on Mount McKinley. He skied so fast that he was out of Alaska and even Canada in a matter of minutes.

Eric did a big telemark turn in snow-covered Bozeman, Montana, jumped off Theodore Roosevelt's nose on Mount Rushmore a few minutes later, felt the weather warming up as he did another wide telemark turn in slushy snow in Chicago, noticed that the snow disappeared when he passed Lincoln Middle School in Edwardsville, Illinois, and landed in the Mississippi River, hoping that it might be a new cross-country ski trail. Unfortunately for Eric, it wasn't. It was the Mississippi River . It was full of Mississippi River water, and it was wet. Eric's long yellow skis kept him afloat just long enough to reach a casino gambling barge floating in the river at St. Louis.

"Do you want to gamble?" asked the people on the gambling boat.

"It's a fin day for skiing," said Eric. "Have you any snow? I would be glad to roll on it and pack it down and teach you all to ski if you say the magic word and give me a few pieces of chocolate." (The magic word was "Please," but not everyone on the gambling boat seemed to know that word, and none of them had extra pieces of chocolate handy.)

A sudden flash of light caught Eric's eye. It was the reflection of the sun on the St. Louis Arch on a hill above the gambling boat. To Eric the Arch looked like the most beautiful snow bridge over a crevasse in a glacier Eric had ever seen. The only things that were missing were the glacier, the crevasse, and the snow. But the Arch looked so slick and steep that Eric was sure it would be just like skiing on the snow on the

Eric the Skier

Matterhorn, something Eric had done many times with plenty of his magic beeswax on his skis.

"Excuse me," said Eric to the people in the gambling boat as they shuffled cards and put coins in machines to see pictures of fruits Eric's sister Erica could see for free while she hiked along the Appalachian Trail. "I don't want to upset anyone. I just want to ski."

Eric got some magic beeswax and a few tons of snow out of his huge green backpack and skied back and forth all day and all night over the top side of the St. Louis Arch. While he was taking things out of his backpack, Eric also took out a moldy Van Houten bar and ate that and some pepperoni with barbecue sauce. Eric burped several times as he skied (always excusing himself, of course), but for Eric, even though the Arch was narrow and steep, the skiing was easy, like the gorges he skied for practice in the Himalayas. He even read passages about the Mississippi River from Huckleberry Finn as he skied.

What Eric really wanted to do was ski the bottom side of the Arch. But Eric did not know how to ski upside down very well. Eric had not been upside down since long ago when his father, the surveyor, played with and held him upside down while he did his surveying. Eric did not know much about math or science since he was always skiing on his desk at school, but he knew enough to know that he would probably fall from the Arch unless he skied at just the right speed. But what was the right speed? Eric did not know.

Eric thought that maybe his family could help him. So Eric put a note in a bottle to float down the Mississippi and out to sea for his brother Alex. Eric was sure Alex would find it somewhere near his home on Color Island. But Eric used a very colorful bottle from the casino just to be sure.

Eric also whispered a message to a bird that was heading north for the spring to give to his sister Erika, who sang and talked with the birds while paddling her tiny birch bark canoe. Eric knew that Erika would be paddling especially fast with all the water from the melting snow.

Eric called his timid sister Edwina from a telephone in the casino. The phone rang thirty-three times before Edwina answered. Edwina was too timid to answer a telephone unless it rang thirty-three times to match the number of locks on her door; she knew a family member was probably calling if the phone rang thirty-three times because anyone else, even an insurance salesperson, would hang up before that. But Edwina was still too scared to talk on the phone herself because she might accidentally talk too fast and get a sore throat, which might lead to a doctor who would give her a shot and then a lollipop with a stick which she might swallow. So Edwina put her gray cat Worrywart on the line.

"Hello, it's a fin day for skiing," said Eric.

"Meow," said the cat.

"Do you know anything about math or arches?" said Eric.

"Meow," said the cat.

Eric the Skier

"I see, "said Eric. "I don't want to upset anyone. I just want to ski the St. Louis Arch," said Eric.

"Meow," concluded the cat.

Eric still did not know about how to ski the bottom side of the arch, but he was very pleased. That had been one of his longest and best telephone calls. Worrywart must have been pleased as well. She purred for the rest of the afternoon while eating cat food out of her crystal glass cat food dish.

Eric called his father and mother. His father was very excited and remembered all the other arches he had surveyed. He told Eric the dimensions of the Arc de Triomphe, the arch in Washington Square, Hadrian's Arch and every McDonald's arch around the world. But he could not tell Eric how fast to ski to stay on the bottom side of the St. Louis Arch. Neither could Eric's mother. But before she started aerobic dancing that afternoon, Eric's mother baked a huge batch of sugar cookies in the shape of arches, a batch almost big enough to fill Eric's huge green backpack. These cookies were very popular when Eric handed them out to everyone on the gambling boat. Most people ate them right away, though a few people tried using them for chips.

Just when he had put a few hundred left-over arch-shaped sugar cookies in his huge green backpack, Eric heard a loud splash. Eric turned around, and there was his brother, Alex. Alex was soaking wet and wearing a bathing suit painted to look like Stan Musial's old St. Louis Cardinal uniform on the front and Dizzy Dean's old uniform on the back.

Alex said hello, shook hands with Eric, ate a sugar cookie, waited twenty minutes before going back into the water, and backstroked for hours up and down a stretch of the Mississippi River next to the Arch. Alex backstroked because it gave him the feeling of being upside down on the Arch and gave him a good view of the bottom of the Arch. Alex backstroked back and forth for hours and hours, but it didn't help him figure out how fast Eric should ski to keep from falling off the bottom of the St. Louis Arch. Except when it came to understanding how much time there was between low tide and high tide, Alex knew even less about math than Eric because he had spent all his time in math class doodling and drawing pictures of fish.

Alex thought of many ways the St. Louis Arch could be painted. Alex kicked and splashed to fill the air with water, creating hundreds of rainbows that looked like the colorful arches he wanted to paint. For a while the City of St. Louis looked like it had not just one Arch but thousands of arches, each more colorful than the last. Even the people on the gambling boat thought the sight of all those colorful arches was beautiful, though not as beautiful as the sight of three yellow lemons in the slot machine. Alex painted many bathing suits with arches and rainbows on them. Some of these are hanging in museums today.

Eric the Skier

Just then Eric heard a beautiful sound, like the tinkling of thousands of bells. Eric turned around and saw his sister Erika paddling up the Mississippi in her birch bark canoe surrounded by thousands of cardinals and other birds, with her long blonde hair streaming behind her on the wind. Erika and the birds were singing the "St. Louis Blues" in voices that sounded like thousands of Billie Holidays and Janice Joplins.

Erika gave her brother Eric a big hug and a few gallons of blueberries from outside Eric's secret cabin in the wood.

"Zank you," said Eric, giving Erika some arch-shaped sugar cookies.

"You're welcome," said Erika, eating some cookies to be polite. but breaking most of them into crumbs to give to her friends, the birds. The birds were tired and hungry from all that singing and trying to fly as fast as Erika could paddle.

Erika paddled up and down the same stretch of the Mississippi Alex had backstroked. She paddled and paddled for hours, looking up at the underside of the Arch high above her. Erika had canoed down many steep waterfalls, even Niagara Falls, but even Erika had never canoed up a waterfall, let alone the bottom of an arch.

"This is a complicated mathematical problem," said Erika.

"Yes," said Eric, "but it's a fin day for skiing."

"Eric, I have an idea," said Erika "Stay right here and eat some blueberries. Alex and I will be back soon."

So Erika paddled off down the Mississippi singing "Meet Me in St. Louis" surrounded by thousands of birds. Alex water-skied and swam behind Erika's canoe. Eric wondered where they were going for a while, but soon, as they usually do, Eric's thoughts turned to skiing and eating. So Eric ate some blueberries from his backpack, had some cookies and pepperoni to go with them, and skied around and around the bottom of the St. Louis Arch for hours. He skied all afternoon and all night under the moonlight and all the next morning and afternoon under a blazing Missouri sun.

People in the gambling boat placed bets on when Eric would stop skiing, but Eric skied so long that no one ever won any of those bets. Eric skied fast and skied slow, skied frontwards and backwards, did figure eights and loop the loops, used old skiing techniques and new skiing techniques — all the long while looking up at the bottom of the Arch above him and wondering whether he would ever get to use any of these techniques there. Skiing around the Arch reminded Eric of times he had skied around the Arc de Triomphe in Paris, although that was more exciting because of the all the traffic through which he had to ski. No one in St. Louis tried to run him over in a Citroen, or honked at him from behind in a Renault, or yelled naughty French words at him while backing a Peugeot over his skis.

Eric the Skier

After skiing exactly thirty-three hours, Eric heard a bell in the distance. It sounded like an old sailing ship's bell. He heard it ring eight times, sounding each time a little closer. Eric looked down the Mississippi, and there he saw a mighty British sailing ship slowly sailing up against the flow of the Mississippi River, with all its sails set and a British flag flapping in the breeze. Erika was canoeing beside the ship and helping to tow it, and Alex was swimming in front of it and helping to guide it. Alex had painted a map of the British Isles on his bathing suit in the ship's honor, and Erika was humming "Hail Britannia" because she did not know the words. Thousands of hummingbirds who also did not know the words flew alongside and hummed along with Erika.

Erika paddled Eric out to the mighty sailing ship. Eric read a nameplate on its stern which said Nonesuch. Eric heard sailors' voices saying things like "hard to starboard," "close haul the mainsail," and "all stays set on the mizzen mast," things which didn't seem to be about skiing and therefore meant nothing to Eric but sounded interesting all the same. Eric and Erika climbed up some ropes to get on board the ship, and Erika introduced Eric to the ship's captain.

"Eric, I would like you to meet Sir Horatio Hornblower, a friend of mine and Alex's who sails all over the world fighting battles and using math all the time to figure out how to capture other ships. He is as good at sailing a great ship as you are at skiing with your great skis. He has agreed to help with mathematical calculations for skiing the bottom of the St. Louis Arch."

Horatio Hornblower was a tall man in a dark blue uniform with several medals. He had a sword at his side and wore a huge, plumed admiral's hat on his head.

"Welcome aboard," said Hornblower with a voice used to giving orders.

"Zank you," said Eric. "This is a beautiful ship. All the wooden planks remind me of thousands of hand-made skis. I have read a lot about you, Sir Hornblower, in books people have left behind at ski lodges. It's a fin day for skiing, even on a ship with no snow on it."

"Excuse me for a few moments," said Hornblower with a bow, "but I must capture the ship across the way for the Royal Navy," pointing to the gambling boat, "and claim St. Louis as a British province."

"But you can't do that," said Alex. "Britain hasn't been at war with the United Sates since the end of the War of 1812."

"Hmmm," said Hornblower.

"The people in St. Louis can't be part of a British province," said Erika. "They already have their own hockey team, baseball team, zoo, museums, symphony orchestra, zip codes, area codes, and parking meters."

Eric the Skier

"Hmmm," said Hornblower.

"And anyway," explained Eric, "the gambling boat doesn't actually sail or go anywhere."

"It's only in a technical sense a boat," said Alex. "The only thing that it does that a boat does is stay in the water."

"It's really not a great ship like yours," concluded Eric," but a tax haven." "Tax haven" was a phrase Eric had seen many times in brochures at ski lodges.

"Ah," exclaimed Hornblower. "I doubt that the British government would want me to bring back a new tax haven. But I must inspect the operations to be sure."

So Hornblower boarded the gambling boat and undertook inspection. For Hornblower, who was an excellent whist player, inspection meant playing several hands of cards. Hornblower was a very good whist player because he knew a lot about math and remembered all the cards played. Hornblower taught everyone on the gambling boat how to play whist and as a result of his inspection ended up with several new American friends and even more new American dollars.

This put Hornblower in a very good mood indeed when he returned to the Nonesuch to spend the evening with Eric. Eric and Hornblower paced the quarterdeck of the Nonesuch for hours, telling each other their adventures, while looking up at the bottom of the Arch as Hornblower did mathematical calculations.

Hornblower always paced the weather side of the quarterdeck when he was thinking. Eric, of course, always skied when he was thinking – or even when he was not thinking. So Eric spread some snow from his huge green knapsack on the quarterdeck of the Nonesuch and skied alongside Hornblower as Hornblower paced and thought. This was some of the most difficult skiing Eric had ever done. The quarterdeck was only twenty-four feet long, and very narrow. Eric had to do many sharp turns and jumps over Hornblower and his huge admiral's hat on his long yellow skis. Every time he and Hornblower had to turn around, which was often, Eric had to be especially careful about his ski poles, and Hornblower had to be especially careful about his ceremonial sword. As it was, there were many little bumps and near misses, and Hornblower and Eric were often saying "Pardon me," By Your Leave," and "After you, sir."

When not apologizing or being apologized to, Hornblower paced and muttered words like "parabola," "centripetal force," and "vectors sufficient to overcome gravity." Eric skied alongside and muttered things like "It's a fin day for skiing" and "I don't want to upset anyone or any ship, I just want to ski."

Eric and Hornblower were up all night skiing and pacing, doing mathematical calculations, and talking about sailing in great wooden sailing ships and skiing on great wooden skis. Eric mentioned the weather

Eric the Skier

and Hornblower suddenly stopped pacing, causing Eric to ski into him. "Aha," said Hornblower at the same time that Eric said, "Pardon me" for the thirty-third time that night.

"It's all right, Eric," said Hornblower. "I think it will be a fine — or as it were, a fin — day for skiing tomorrow if the wind blows a fair quarter from the West, as I believe it will. The speed at which you must ski to stay on the bottom of the Arch is a constant fifteen knots. Any more or less and you will fall right off."

Eric could pretty well ski any speed he wanted any time he wanted, but he had no idea of what a knot was except as something he put in a rope if he was rescuing an injured skier on an emergency sled. Hornblower tried to explain what a knot was in terms of miles per hour, but it was like trying to explain to Edwina that she did not have to be afraid of something. Edwina always ended up being afraid. Eric ended up thinking of things on the end of ropes. The more he heard about miles per hour, the more tangled the ropes got in Eric's imagination. Finally Hornblower measured Eric's skis and explained to Eric how many times he should move his skis per minute: thirty-three times. Thirty-three glides a minute would be impossible for anyone else, especially with skis as long and heavy as Eric's, but for Eric it was easy. In fact Eric demonstrated how easy it was for Hornblower. Unfortunately, Eric forgot he was on the twenty-four foot long quarterdeck of a sailing ship and skied into the mizzenmast, causing many sailors to think that the Nonesuch had hit an unexpected iceberg in the Mississippi River.

Hornblower explained that if Eric glided exactly thirty-three times per minute with his skis and if he had a sail on his back to catch exactly 3.3 knots of wind from the West, he could just barely ski the bottom of the St. Louis Arch without falling off.

Dawn was just breaking over the yardarm as several sailors finished sewing up a sail they rigged to Eric's backpack. Then, as Hornblower had thought, a faint breeze began to blow from the West. Alex treaded water in one part of the Mississippi, Erika paddled in circles in another, and the lifeboats from the Nonesuch rowed to a third place to be able to rescue Eric if he should fall. Soon the breeze blew harder, Hornblower fiddled with the ropes, Eric put extra beeswax on the bottom of his skis, and the little sail on Eric's huge green backpack puffed out with air as the wind speed reached exactly 3.3 knots an hour.

"Off you go, Eric," said Hornblower. "Godspeed and good luck."

"It's a fin day for skiing upside down," said Eric.

And off Eric went, skiing exactly thirty-three strides a minute on his long yellow skis while the sail on his backpack filled with the breeze from the West.

At first it was indeed a fin day for skiing. Up Eric skied, upside down. Up and up and up. He concentrated hard on gliding thirty-three

Eric the Skier

times a minute with his skis. People from the gambling boat came outside and held their breath as they watched Eric ski up and up the great Arch of St. Louis.

Just as Eric was reaching the top, the wind died down. A hush fell on the crowd. Even Erika stopped singing. If the wind were less than 3.3 knots, even for a few seconds, Eric would fall hundreds of feet and injure himself as well as his skis and the blueberries in his backpack.

Hornblower stopped fiddling with the ropes and started pacing.

"Aha," he cried. "Blow, you men, blow."

All the sailors started blowing in the direction of Eric. They blew as hard as if they were blowing up hundreds of birthday balloons. Then Alex and Erika and Hornblower himself blew. The people from the gambling boat blew. People all over St. Louis began to blow and blow. Papers flew everywhere. But sure enough, the sail on Eric's back, which had gone slack for a second, filled again with air and Eric skied on. Soon the wind picked up again, the people stopped blowing and panted for breath, and Eric schussed down the St. Louis Arch and came to a stop right at its base.

"Hip, hip, hooray!" shouted Hornblower.

Alex and Erika, the sailors, the people from the gambling boat — in fact, all the people in St. Louis—cheered as loudly as they could. Fortunately for their eardrums, that wasn't very loudly because they were all still out of breath. Even Erika was out of breath. But the cheering was loud enough to make Eric happy and proud and so fond of the City of St. Louis that he put a snow globe of it in his secret cabin in the woods.

Horatio Hornblower got ready to sail his great ship the Nonesuch back down the Mississippi.

"Zank you for all you have done," said Eric. Eric gave Hornblower a huge bag of his magic beeswax and told Hornblower how to put it on the hull of the Nonesuch. Eric knew it would make the ship sail even faster and patch up leaks from cannonballs and hurricanes. Although Eric did not say so, it also made the ship smell a good deal better below decks when it was at sea for months at a time. Eric also gave Hornblower a ceremonial ski pole to go along with Hornblower's ceremonial sword.

Hornblower made Eric an honorary midshipman in the British Navy and gave him the job of inspecting all snow before it turned into water and became the oceans on which the British Navy would sail. Hornblower said that because pollution and climate change were making the world warmer, more and more snow was turning into water and Eric's duties as midshipman in charge of snow would be increasing and would be more and more important. Eric was a proud honorary midshipman, but also, of course, a sad one as he thought of all the melting snow.

"It's a fin day for skiing, isn't it, Eric?" shouted Hornblower as the great sails on his great sailing ship flapped and filled with air, and the Nonesuch started down the Mississippi.

"Aye, aye, sir," shouted Midshipman Eric with a crisp salute.

The ship looked as colorful as if Alex had painted it. In fact, he did paint the Nonesuch on several bathing suits when he got back to Color Island. Some of them are hanging in museums today. The great sails slowly disappeared in the sunset as the Nonesuch sailed down the Mississippi and into the Gulf of Mexico with Alex water skiing behind it and Erika leading the way in her birch bark canoe. Erika had caught her breath and sang "You've come a long way from St. Louis" in a voice that could fill many jazz clubs, as her long blond hair spread out behind her like a banner on the wind.

Eric looked on for a few minutes and then turned north in search of snow. What else would Eric do, especially now with his new responsibilities as Midshipman in Charge of Snow for the British Royal Navy?

James Kobak

Eric the Skier Goes to the Hospital

Eric the Skier woke up one day with a sharp pain in his stomach. Could the pain be from eating too much pepperoni, wondered Eric, chewing on a piece of pepperoni? This had never happened before, and Eric had eaten a lot of pepperonis, as well as many other things. Eric opened his giant green backpack and swallowed some of his magic beeswax. The beeswax could fix almost anything, but it could not fix Eric's stomachache. Eric decided that he needed to see a doctor. So Eric put on his long yellow skis and skied and skied until he came to a small hospital in Littleton, New Hampshire.

Eric skied inside the hospital and very politely told the nurses and doctors that he didn't want to upset anyone, he just wanted to ski, but that he had a pain in his stomach that did not go away no matter how fast he skied or what techniques he used.

The doctors poked at Eric, the nurses pinched him, and they all asked him where things hurt, but Eric was as polite as usual and simply answered, "Zankyou. It's a fin day for skiing."

The doctors gave Eric X-rays and bone scans. The nurses gave him blood tests and took his temperature when the hospital ran out of other tests to do.

Finally, the doctor in charge of the hospital shook hands with Eric and said,

"Welcome. I am afraid you have appendicitis and we have to take out your appendix. It's not something you need for skiing or for doing anything else, for that matter. Your stomach and everything else look fine, although your stomach does have more cookies and pieces of pepperoni in it than any of our machines can count. We have to do a simple operation called an appendectomy. You should feel fine, but may not be able to ski for a few days."

Eric tried to look cheerful, but not being able to ski for even a day or two was almost as sad for Eric as melting snow.

"Can I keep my skis on for the operation?," asked Eric.

Eric the Skier

"Your skis are awfully long, but fortunately, we have a new roof with very high ceilings, so that should be all right," said the doctor. "Who knows, Eric? You might even dream about skiing during the operation," added the doctor, to cheer Eric up.

"Do you use long yellow skis when you operate?" asked Eric.

"Well, no, but I do use long yellow surgical tools," said the doctor.

"Do you coat them with beeswax from secret hiding places in the woods?" asked Eric.

"Well, no, they didn't teach me about that in medical school. But I guess I could try," said the doctor.

The doctor then showed Eric his yellow surgical tools. Several of them reminded Eric of ski poles or waxing tools and made him feel much better. The doctor explained the operation to Eric, showing him how he would move the tools this way and that during the operation and where the sharp turns and places to stop were.

"This is just like the famous Holmenkollen skiing trails in Norway, said Eric.

"I suppose so," said the doctor." "I don't know much about skiing. I just want to make other people feel better."

"We should call this an appendecto-ski, not an appendectomy," said Erick.

"I suppose so," said the doctor. "It will be the first appendecto-ski in medical history."

"And it will be fin day for appendecto-skiing," concluded Eric.

While Eric and the doctor were talking, Erika heard about Erik's stomachache from a bluebird that had seen Eric ski into the hospital. Erika sent the bluebird to tell the rest of the family and paddled to the hospital in no time in her birch bark canoe, cascading down flumes, waterfalls, and rapids, surrounded by birds with her long blond hair streaming behind her like a banner in the wind. Erica and the birds sang "The Hip Bone's Connected to the Tailbone" so beautifully that it sounded like an opera.

Alex learned about Eric's stomachache from a mako shark who had heard about it from a sea gull who had talked to the blue bird. Alex put a note in a bottle and asked a dolphin to deliver it to Erik's mother and father. Alex backstroked and surfed in the Gulf Stream from Color Island to the hospital almost as fast as Erika paddled, drawing pictures from Gray's Anatomy on his bathing suit.

Edwina leaned about Eric's stomachache from her pet cat Worrywart, who had talked to the bluebird. It took Edwina some time to get to the hospital. First, she had to put on her best gray dress, hat, and shoes; then she had to worry about whether to bring an umbrella or not. Then Edwina had to put food in Worrywart's crystal glass cat food dish, which meant worrying about whether the food was too much or too little. Edwina had to decide whether to put on an overcoat or not; whether to leave a light on or off; whether to turn the heat in her gray apartment up or down. Then Edwina had to unlock all thirty-three locks on her apartment door and lock them all up again and worry whether she had all thirty-three keys. And of course she had to worry about train schedules, bus schedules, subway schedules, airline schedules, ferry boat schedules, taxicabs, Uber drivers, bicycles, red lights, green lights, yellow lights, stop signs and one way streets, to say nothing of possible earthquakes, avalanches, and unpredicted eclipses of the sun. The one good thing about all this worry was that it left Edwina almost no time to worry about Eric.

When she got to the hospital, Erika had to leave her birch bark canoe in the hospital parking lot. The birds also had to stay outside, but the hospital recorded their singing for the patients. Erika brought a basket of colorful wildflowers into the hospital waiting room.

When Alex got to the hospital, he had to leave his surfboard in the parking lot and had to wear a gown over his bathing suit. Alex promptly painted a picture of a bathing suit with scenes from the television show E.R. on the gown so that he would feel more at home. Alex brought a beach bucket full of colorful seaweeds and periwinkle shells into the waiting room.

Edwina had mustered all her courage and brought a large gray lollipop into the waiting room, though she was deathly afraid that Eric might swallow it and have to see another doctor and go to another hospital and have another operation and end up with yet another lollipop which he might also swallow.

Eric's mother had heard about Eric's operation on public radio and was already in the waiting room, pretending to do aerobic dancing but really hoping that Eric would be all right. Eric's father was also in the waiting room, pretending to survey the couches and chair but also really hoping that Eric would be all right.

The doctor took out his yellow surgical tools and covered some of them with Eric's magic beeswax. He did the operation easily and very fast, much as if he were Eric skiing the Hollmenkollen ski trails. And Eric did dream about skiing the whole time. After all, what else would Eric have to dream about?

Eric dreamed he was skiing in Canada, in Switzerland, and in Norway all at once. He dreamed he was skiing on perfectly groomed ski trails and rugged, trailless backcountry terrain all at once. In his dream Eric skied up avalanches and down volcanoes at the same time. He heard Erika and the birds singing many different kinds of music, all of it more beautiful than any music he had ever heard before. He dreamed he was skiing through art galleries and museums where Alex's most colorful bathing suits hung on every wall. Eric dreamed he was skiing aerobically with his mother and surveying mountain ranges with his father. Eric dreamed he skied slowly through a great gray canyon with Edwina on one shoulder and Worrywart on the other. Eric even dreamed about people

Eric the Skier

working together to stop global warming so that Eric could keep skiing in all these places in real life, not just in his dreams.

This was a lot of dreaming about skiing, even for Eric, and when he awoke, he was tired. He was surprised to find himself in a hospital bed surrounded by doctors, nurses and his family members. He thought he would be in the beautiful Northern woods, surrounded by his friends, the forest creatures. With all the flowers, seaweed, and shells, to say nothing of a large gray lollipop, the room looked and smelled just as beautiful. And the smiles of his family made it more beautiful still.

"How are you, Eric?" asked everyone, including the nurses and doctors, all at once. "How do you feel? Are you in any pain?"

"It was a fin day for appendecto-skiing," said Eric.

"Do you need anything?" said several voices all at once.

"No, zankyou, said Eric. "I don't need anything but snow. I don't want to upset anyone. I just want to ski,"

"You didn't happen to swallow any lollipops, did you?" said a timid voice in the corner that Eric was pretty sure was Edwina's.

"No, but that big gray lollipop looks pretty tasty. I will eat that with a few pieces of pepperoni when I am back out on the trail."

And with that Eric drifted back to sleep and dreamt about endless snowfields and mile after mile of fresh new snow.

Within a few days Eric was as good as new and a better skier than ever because of all the places he had learned to ski through his dreams. Eric spread snow from his huge green backpack on some of the hospital corridors and taught doctors and nurses and even several patients to become expert skiers – everyone except Eric's doctor, who spent all his time thinking about new operations, just as Eric spends all his time thinking about new places to ski.

When Eric left the hospital, Erica gave the doctors and nurses a huge bowl of blueberries to share. Alex gave the doctor a bathing suit with a picture of the doctor that made him look like Dr. Kildare. The picture now hangs in the hospital waiting room. Edwina was too worried about her apartment and her pet cat Worrywart to stay for long, but she left behind thirty-three lollipops. Eric's mother baked hundreds of cookies, which everyone in the hospital ate, even those who were supposed to be on diets. Eric's father did a complete survey of the hospital, which hangs in the waiting room next to Alex's bathing suit painting.

Eric hugged all of his family members and the nurses and shook hands with the doctor.

"Zank you very much," said Eric.

"You are welcome," said the doctor. "And thank you for the magic beeswax. I am going to use it in all operations from now on and write up how to use it for an appendecto-ski for a medical journal. Do you have any questions?"

"Just one," said Eric. "Which way is north?"

The doctor consulted with Eric's father and pointed the way. And with that Eric gathered some of Erika's blueberries, Alex's seaweed, Edwina's gray lollipop, and a few pounds of fresh pepperoni from the hospital cafeteria and put them in his huge green backpack along with a few hundred of his mother's cookies. This should be enough to tide me over until lunch, thought Eric, who was clearly feeling like his old self again.

Eric skied out of the hospital with his huge green backpack on his back. Eric had a huge grin on his face, and massive amounts of cookies and pepperoni in his pockets for his friends, the forest creatures.

"Bon voyage," said the doctor.

"It's a fin day for skiing after all," replied Eric, who was soon a dot in the distance as he sped away, heading North through the warming earth, hoping still to find fresh snow in the places he had dreamed about during his operation.

James Kobak

Edwina and Her Bicycle

Edwina almost never read newspapers, watched her gray television, listened to her gray radio, or looked at blogs on her gray computer because she was too worried about the new problems and disasters that she might learn about. Instead, Edwina cowered under her gray comforter and worried about what might be on the news. One day, however, Edwina under her gray comforter received a postcard by carrier pigeon from her brother Eric, noting that it was a fin day for skiing but that the glaciers were shorter and the snow less deep than Eric could ever remember—and if there was anything Eric could remember exactly, it was snow conditions.

The next day Edwina received a singing telegram from her sister Erika, telling her how beautiful the woods still were even though the trees were shorter and drier and there was more smoke from wildfires. And the day after that Edwina found a waterlogged envelope in her mailbox containing a letter written in thirty-three colors with many illustrations by Alex; although a little smudged, Alex's pictures and words showed that the world's oceans were still a beautiful blue color but seemed to have fewer fish and smaller coral reefs. Then Edwina's father telegraphed that he was starting to run out of ice to survey in Antarctica but had plenty of new desert sand to work on in Africa. And Edwina's mother left a message on Edwina's gray telephone (that Edwina finally had the courage to pick up after thirty-three rings) saying that Edwina's mother had to go to more meetings than ever about something called global warming.

Now Edwina had something new and serious to worry about along with all the old and silly things she already spent all her time worrying about. This was a new level of worrying for Edwina. She furrowed her brow, pursed her lips, clenched her fists, and worried and worried under her gray comforter until gray steam almost seemed to seep out of her ears. Edwina worried so hard that she forgot to pet her gray cat Worrywart. She would even have forgotten to feed Worrywart had that famous gray cat not said "Meow" loudly enough to rattle the oatmeal bowls in Edwina's gray cupboards.

Edwina worried and worried and worried. Edwina worried so much that she soon had a headache. And a stomachache. And a backache. And an arm ache, a leg ache, a nose ache and a little toe ache.

Edwina had so many aches that she decided that she would have to go to the doctor. Of course, Edwina was very reluctant to see any doctor because of what she worried what might happen: the doctor might give her a shot that might hurt, and then the doctor might give Edwina a lollipop with a lollipop stick that she might swallow. And then who knew what might happen?

But Edwina finally took a deep breath, threw off her gray comforter, gathered Worrywart in her arms and unlocked all thirty-three locks on her apartment door. She squinted as she opened the door and crept along the city streets and sidewalks dressed in her gray summer dress in the bright sunshine on one of the hottest days of the year.

"I'm rather hot," thought Edwina to herself, and Worrywart under all the gray fur seemed to agree.

"I hope my feet don't melt," Edwina continued thinking to herself, "because that might hurt and would ruin my gray shoes and might leave me in the middle of the street. Then I might get hit by that school bus on the corner or that car on the next block, or a motorcycle ten blocks away, or a van from Pennsylvania, a truck from Indiana, an RV from Arizona, or a motor scooter from Italy." Worrywart under all that gray fur seemed to agree, though it was hard to tell because somewhere between Indiana and Arizona the famous gray cat had fallen asleep.

When Edwina crept into the doctor's office, the doctor asked the new patient, who seemed rather worried and nervous, what she did for a living.

"Mostly I worry," said Edwina.

"What do you do for hobbies?" asked the doctor.

"I worry about new things and old things. I'm sort of a collector of things to worry about," said Edwina.

"What do you do when you're not worrying?" asked the doctor.

Edwina had to pause to think, but finally she said, "I sleep. But then my dreams wake me up, and I start to worry again."

"I see you are a worrywart," said the doctor.

"I beg your pardon," said Edwina. "I am not a cat."

"Meow," said Worrywart when she thought she heard her name and food might be involved.

"I'm glad you let me know," said the doctor, "because I'm not a veterinarian and you can't be too sure. But I think I know just what you need, something to cheer you up and get your mind off your troubles."

Eric the Skier

And the doctor started to take a large lollipop as colorful as one of Alex's bathing suits out of one of his pockets.

This did not cheer up Edwina one bit. Edwina knew what might happen now. She might swallow the lollipop stick, get shots, and all the rest. So she picked up Worrywart and ran out of the office and down thirty-three flights of stairs. The doctors, the nurses, the receptionist, and one patient with a sweet tooth who had seen the lollipop, all ran after her. Edwina was so terrified that all her worries had come true that she almost forgot to worry. She ran and ran, and so did the doctor and nurses, the receptionist, and the hungry patient. As Edwina ran, the lollipop stick grew larger and larger in her imagination until it seemed to be the size of the Eiffel Tower or a skyscraper.

Edwina ran out the door with Worrywart in her arms, and there, right outside the door, was a bicycle. She gave its owner her life savings, which consisted largely of ten-cent-off supermarket coupons for oatmeal purchases and several cans of gray paint. Then Edwina jumped on the bicycle and started pedaling. She pedaled faster and faster even though she worried that the bicycle was in the wrong gear and might have flat tires and broken brakes. The doctor and nurses and even the hungry patient all gave up running after a block or two, but Edwina worried they would catch her, and she pedaled faster and faster and faster. Edwina pedaled so hard that even Worrywart woke up for a few minutes. Edwina worried about traffic, about flat tires, about gears that might not work, pedals that might fall off, brakes that would stop her too suddenly or not stop her at all, about staying on the bicycle forever and falling off the bicycle at any moment.

The more Edwina worried, the faster she pedaled. This was the most worrying even Edwina had ever done at one time. The breeze and the exercise made it almost fun to be worrying and reminded Edwina of the times as a child she had had gone down waterfalls with Erika in Erika's birch bark canoe. But then Edwina worried that if she were almost having fun, she must not be worrying enough, and all the things she must be forgetting to worry about would come true.

Edwina worried so hard that she bicycled faster than traffic. She bicycled faster than other bicyclists in colorful uniforms that looked as if they had been painted by Alex. People stood beside the roads as Edwina sped by and waved signs and cheered in French and many other languages because Edwina was actually winning the Tour de France bicycle race, climbing up mountain passes like the Alpe d'Huez much faster than Christopher Froome and whooshing by sprinters on flat roads in world record time. But to Edwina all the people cheering were French doctors and medical students clamoring to give her a shot, and all the signs looked like fancy lollipops designed by famous French pastry chefs. So Edwina pedaled even faster.

Edwina pedaled so fast that for a while she became a great gray blur of worry. The blur sped through cities, towns and villages like a

Eric the Skier

cyclone or tornado with a whirring noise and an occasional "Meow." Trees swayed, flagpoles flapped and kites flew high in the air as the gray blur of the worrying Edwina on a bicycle flew past. When Edwina pedaled through high mountains Eric tried to keep up with her on his long yellow skis, but even with all the magic beeswax from his huge green backpack Eric could not keep up with that great gray blur of worry. Eric couldn't slow Edwina down, no matter how often he tried to remind her that he didn't want to upset anyone, he just wanted to ski.

Erika tried to keep up with Edwina in her tiny birch bark canoe when the great gray blur of worry pedaled on roads beside rivers like the Mississippi and the Amazon. But even Erika paddling down a waterfall could not canoe fast enough. To calm Edwina, Erika and her friends, the birds, sang lullabies Erika's mother used to sing at the end of aerobic dancing classes, but the songs were lost in the whir of the pedals.

Alex surfed faster than Mark Phelps can swim. But even Alex and the fastest dolphins in the ocean could not keep up with Edwina when that great gray blur of worry pedaled on ocean beaches, scattering crabs and causing sailboats to rock at their moorings. All Alex could do was paint a new bathing suit in thirty-three shades of gray in honor of the great gray blur of worried sister he saw speeding away like a cyclone or tornado.

Pedaling so fast took a lot of energy, and eventually even Edwina, despite all the nervous energy caused by worrying, began to slow down. Edwina also realized that she was getting hungry. Worrywart seemed to agree, with an especially loud "Meow." It was unanimous: time to have some oatmeal. No doctors or lollipops appeared to be in the vicinity. So Edwina stopped pedaling and went from being a gray blur to a gray streak to a gray bicyclist going faster than cars and trucks to a slow gray bicyclist to a person dressed in gray getting off a bicycle in front of an apartment building with a gray cat in one hand and the keys to thirty-three locks in the other.

After Edwina and Worrywart had had some oatmeal and Edwina was sure she had not swallowed some the wrong way, and after Edwina had checked under her gray bed and her gray comforter to be sure there were no hidden doctors or lollipops, and after Edwina had cleaned Worrywart's crystal glass cat food dish and had checked all the thirty-three locks on her apartment door, and after Worrywart yawned several times, Edwina and Worrywart went to sleep. Edwina dreamed of flying along on her bicycle with the wind in her hair and thought how beautiful it was, but also how scary it was. Even in her dream Edwina worried about how she might have fallen off the bicycle on a hairpin turn or a hill or even a playground where toddlers rode their big wheels and tricycles. Edwina also remembered, even while she was dreaming, that she had worried about global warming and worried that for a few minutes she may have forgotten to worry about something she should have been worrying about. So, of course, Edwina woke up worried. Worrywart, of course, woke up saying, "Meow."

Eric the Skier

Edwina worried and worried and soon wanted to bicycle some more. But now Edwina was too worried to bicycle outdoors where there were hills, valleys, robbers, and pirates, and of course doctors with lollipops who might be lurking on any street corner. Yet there was still global warming to worry about, to say nothing of wars and avalanches and volcanoes and broken locks and oatmeal shortages.

So Edwina decided to keep riding her bicycle—but only inside her apartment. Edwina pedaled between the gray bed and the gray cupboards holding Edwina's oatmeal dishes and the gray telephone she almost never answered and the door with thirty-three locks. She pedaled thirty-three times clockwise around her apartment, often bumping into her bed. She pedaled around the apartment counterclockwise thirty-three times, sometimes bumping into her cupboards. She bumped into Worrywart once or twice, causing loud "Meows."

There were a few dents in the bed and the cupboards by the time Edwina finished pedaling for the day, to say nothing of a few bruises on Edwina's shins (though only small bruises that only needed a gray band-aid or two and fortunately none that meant she would have to visit a doctor with the risk of shots and lollipops and all the rest). There may even have been a dent or two in Worrywart's gray whiskers, although, since all Worrywart said was "Meow," it was hard to tell.

The pedaling made Edwina feel good, but a little tired. So she and Worrywart had a midnight snack of oatmeal and then Edwina went to bed.

It was cozy under her huge gray comforter with Worrywart nearby saying "Meow" from time to time as she talked in her sleep. Edwina dreamed for a while about riding her bicycle, and then she dreamed about adventures that the members of her family were probably having. But Edwina was still Edwina, and after a while worries began creeping into her dreams. There were all the old little worries about doctors and visitors who might be pirates and supermarkets that might run out of oatmeal. But now there was a newer, much bigger worry: climate change and what it was doing to the earth and all the places where her family had their adventures. So when she was not pedaling her bicycle around the apartment, Edwin sat in her gray apartment worrying.

There sat Edwina huddled under her huge gray comforter, worrying next to her gray cat, Worrywart. All her pedaling had given Edwina more energy with which to worry. And she needed that energy because now she had something that was a hard and important problem to worry about. "I'm worried about what is happening to the world around us," thought Edwina to herself as soon as she woke up in the morning. "Meow" and "I could use a little more oatmeal," thought Worrywart to herself, since it was almost time for breakfast.

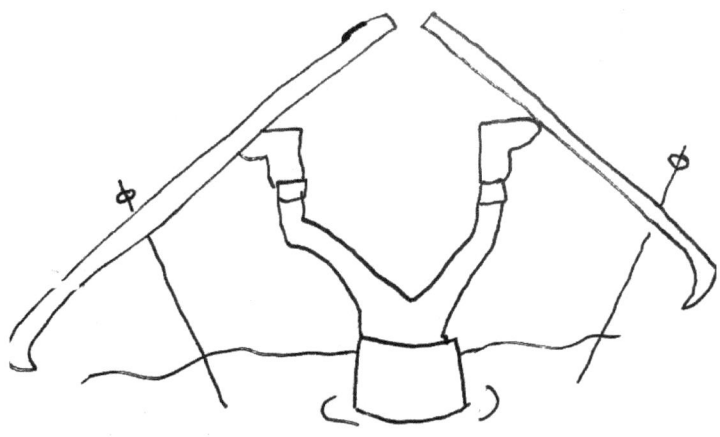

Edwina's Birthday Surprise

While Edwina went from worrying in her gray apartment to pedaling around it and then went back to worrying again, the rest of her family began to worry as well. They worried about Edwina pedaling her bike inside her apartment and bumping into things. And they began to worry themselves about the one thing that Edwina seemed most worried about. And that was global warming.

Eric worried because it was taking him longer and longer to find snow even with his sensitive ski-jump nose, and the snow he did find seemed less deep than before under his long yellow skis. Erika worried because the blueberries seemed to be getting smaller when she hiked uphill, and fewer birds seemed to be flying beside her as she canoed down waterfalls in her birch bark canoe. Alex worried because the water he swam through in his colorful bathing suits seemed warmer than before, and some of his friends, the fish, said they were not feeling very well. A few octopi even reminded Alex of Eric when he had to go to the hospital. Eric's father worried that places he had surveyed before were turning into deserts that he would have to survey again. Eric's mother worried that some of her students seemed to get tired sooner from their aerobic dancing and that it seemed warmer when she danced outside.

Erika paddled her canoe and hiked uphill until she reached Eric's secret cabin in the woods to tell Eric what she was worried about. Eric said he was worried, too, and started to describe melting snowfields with almost as many tears in his eyes as there were drops of melting water. Strange as it seems to say, Eric had a bruise or two from falling headfirst into the snow. Once or twice tips of his long yellow skis had run into rocks and tree roots in bare spots Eric he had never seen before in some of his favorite snowfields.

"We might be worrying too much, "said Eric.

"We might not be worrying enough," said Erika.

"Maybe we are right to worry," said Eric.

"Maybe we should be worrying as much as Edwina," said Erika.

Eric the Skier

Maybe for once Edwina was worrying about something important that everyone should be worrying about, thought Eric and Erika at the same time.

Eric and Erica decided they should talk to Alex about Edwina's worrying and their own worrying. So Eric and Erika headed downhill in the direction of Color Island. Eric couldn't always find snow on the hillsides so he had to ride with Erika down waterfalls in her birch bark canoe. Only now there wasn't much water in some of the waterfalls. Eric and Erika had to carry the canoe down some of the streams, and it wasn't easy for Eric to get down dry streambeds full of rocks and boulders on his long yellow skis. But finally they reached the ocean and paddled to Color Island. Erika sang "It takes a worried man to sing a worried song." Her long blond hair was streaming like a banner in the wind, but she was surrounded by fewer of her friends the birds than usual, and some of them were singing off key--or even screeching as if they were in a Heavy Metal band. When the canoe reached Color Island, it was as colorful as ever, but seemed a little smaller and to have fewer nearby coral reefs than before.

"I had been worrying about Edwina's pedaling so much inside her apartment, but then I thought about what she was worrying about and started worrying about that. Now I am also worrying that I might be worrying too much," said Alex. Alex showed Eric and Erika the brown bathing suits he had started to paint with portraits of whales and jellyfish with frowns on their faces. "I think I am worrying almost as much as

Edwina." Eric and Erika told Alex that they were worrying that much, too. "Maybe for once Edwina is worrying about something important that everyone should be worrying about," said Alex. And of course Eric and Erika shook their heads and said "Yes" to show that they agreed.

Since Edwina was such an expert at worrying, and since they were still worried about her bumping into things as she pedaled her bicycle around her apartment, Eric, Erika, and Alex decided they should visit her. Now Edwina is not the easiest person to visit because of all the locks on her door. You can't just drop by one afternoon. You can't just call up and invite her for lunch because she probably wouldn't answer the phone or would be afraid the menu wouldn't include oatmeal. Even for the members of her family (whom Edwina loves and is always worrying about) it takes a lot of planning to visit Edwina. So Eric, Erika, and Alex spent all January and February planning. This was a lot of planning, especially for Eric. But they knew March 15 was coming and that was Edwina's birthday. So what they planned was a surprise birthday party. And a surprise birthday gift.

The only other guests invited to the party were Eric's mother and father because Edwina would be too worried about having any other people in her apartment. Eric, Erika, and Alex called it a BYOS or Bring Your Own Something party because Edwina would be too worried about anything else being delivered to her apartment and it would spoil the surprise. For Eric it was a BYOSP party—Bring Your Own Snow and

Pepperoni. For Erika it was a BYOCB party—Bring Your Own Canoe and Blueberries. For Alex it was a BYOPB party—Bring Your Own Paint and Bathing Suits. For Eric's mother and father it was a BYOCST party—Bring Your Own Cookies and Surveying Tools. If Edwina knew about it, it would have been a BYOWC party—Bring Your Own Worrywart and Comforter. But of course Edwina wasn't told to bring anything because it was supposed to be a surprise and Worrywart and her huge gray comforter were in the apartment already.

Getting into Edwina's apartment on March 15 wasn't as hard as Eric and the rest of his family thought it might be. They only had to answer thirty-three questions so Edwina was sure they were not robbers, murderers, or pirates and had not gone to medical or lollipop-making school. Then they only had to wait another twenty minutes while Edwina unlocked all thirty-three locks on her door. "Surprise!" and "Happy birthday, Edwina," they all said at the same time when Edwina finally opened the door. They had gray balloons in their hands and gray birthday hats on their heads. Then they threw gray confetti into the air and blew on their gray noisemakers.

Edwina had scarcely begun to worry about balloons on the ceiling, confetti on the floor, and earaches from hearing the noisemakers when the family said, "Surprise" again and Eric took Erika's surprise birthday present out of his huge green backpack. Edwina's birthday surprise was four feet high and covered in gray wrapping paper. Edwina worried that it might be nuclear waste, a crouching mountain lion ready to pounce on Worrywart, or even worse, a crouching doctor ready to pounce on Edwina with a lollipop in his hand. Then she worried that it might be something new to worry about, like an off-course meteor or a spaceship full of tiny Martians. But finally the family blew the noisemakers so loudly that Edwina opened her present.

What Edwina saw under the gray wrapping paper was not nuclear waste or a wild animal. It was not a doctor with a lollipop or something from outer space. Rather, it was a beautiful, gleaming, stationary bicycle. The bicycle had been painted hundreds of vivid colors by Alex on Color Island. It was the only colorful item (apart from the painted oatmeal bowls in her cupboards and the rest of her family) to be seen in Edwina's apartment. The birthday surprise smelled beautiful because it rested on a base of balsam boughs Erika had gathered from fallen trees in the deepest parts of forests all over the world. Its wheels spun fast and noiselessly because Eric had covered them with magic beeswax from his secret hive of bees hidden in a meadow high on the side of a mountain.

While Edwina was opening the surprise, her father had surveyed the apartment to find the perfect place for the stationary bicycle. While he was at it, Edwina's father surveyed Edwina's bathtub, sink, and cupboards and had started to survey Worrywart until stopped by a "Meow" louder than the sound of the noisemakers. Edwina's mother wrote a book of aerobic bicycle-pedaling routines and cooked an oatmeal birthday cake in the shape of a giant bicycle seat. Edwina stopped worrying long enough to say thank you, kiss everyone in her family, and get on her colorful stationary bicycle. Then she began pedaling, and a smile spread across her face. Worrywart smiled, too, and then jumped into Edwina's arms and licked a piece of oatmeal birthday cake off her cheek.

But the surprise was not over yet. For the bicycle had many cords and wires attached to it, and these glowed brighter and brighter with more and more energy the faster Edwina pedaled. Eric explained that he was taking one of the cables and skiing through the Alps, the Pyrenees, and the Dolomites to connect it to powerhouses that would run on the energy from Edwina's pedaling and create no pollution. Eric also put a huge solar panel on his huge green backpack so that the ski lodges where he sometimes stayed would be warm and cozy without causing any pollution.

Erika then picked up a wire and announced that she was hiking and paddling through the Rockies and the Andes to hook up Edwina's energy from worrying and pedaling to office buildings, schoolhouses, and hotels. Alex picked up another wire that glowed a particularly bright crimson and said that he would surf, water ski and back float with it through the Atlantic, Pacific, and Indian oceans and then plug it into factories and railroads in China. (Fortunately, it was a worry energy wire and not an electrical energy wire or Alex would have electrocuted himself and many fish.)

It was a wonderful party. Alex painted decorations in hundreds of shades of gray. Erika sang "Shades of Gray" while her mother danced and taught Edwina aerobic pedaling routines for the stationary bicycle. Eric took snow from his green backpack to keep the oatmeal-flavored ice cream cold. Eric's father surveyed the birthday cake before and after it was covered with the ice cream. And Edwina, after catching her breath from all the pedaling she was doing, announced that she had already worried enough about everybody while opening the thirty-three locks on her door that everybody could relax and have a good time. And so everybody did, including Worrywart, who was careful to stay far away from the stationary bicycle, whiskers and all.

"This was such a wonderful party and wonderful surprise," said Edwina, as her family took down the gray balloons and gray decorations for recycling and swept several tons of gray confetti from the floor to be reused at other parties. "But I am still worried about all that needs to be done to save the world around us and to keep it beautiful that even I might once in a while want to leave my apartment and bicycle through it again."

"You are right to be worried," said Edwina's father. " I have seen damage in more and more of the things I survey and measure. Your mother and I and many others were far too careless for far too long and now we are getting too old to do enough to fix it ourselves. But people everywhere must keep trying. They must keep surveying and measuring to learn what is happening so they will know what to do about it before it is too late."

"Yes," said Eric's mother, "and people must not sit around moping about it or pretending not to notice. They must get up and start doing something about it. It will take a lot of willpower and energy, like aerobic dancing, but it will make people feel better when they have done it, which is also like aerobic dancing. And it will benefit everyone, not just themselves. It is like baking an oatmeal cookie for everyone in the world."

Edwina furrowed her brow and thought about her worrying. Now her worrying was more organized. For example, worries about hurricanes and floods made her think about all the energy in wind and water. Worries about eroding land and mudslides made her think of how trees and plants can protect us. Worries about sunburn gave her ideas about using the power of the sun.

And now, though Edwina usually worried about speaking up too much so that she often stayed silent, speak up she did.

"Everyone," she said, "it is time to get to work. Alex, study the sea and the surf. Find out from the fish what they are feeling. Paint what you learn, paint it everywhere, over and over so that people will know and understand."

"Erika," said Edwina, "Study the trees and the streams and the blueberry bushes and other plants. Ask the birds to tell you what is happening to them. Sing song after song about all you learn so that people everywhere may know and understand."

"Eric," said Edwina, "study the snowfall and glaciers. Learn from the bear and the deer what is happening to them. Tell everyone you meet on your travels. Let them know how to help. I will write thousands of brochures and postcards with instructions for you to put in your huge green backpack and hand out to all the people you meet at ski lodges and meatpacking plants,"

Soon people from all over the world were writing to Edwina for advice and instructions and to ask her to come to meetings. Edwina answered the letters during the day and went to the meetings in the evenings. She went to more meetings than even her mother. She was so busy that she had no time to worry about anything other than answering peoples' questions and telling them what to do next. When she wasn't eating oatmeal, she even sucked on a lollipop from time to time so she wouldn't get hungry at meetings.

Solar power panels and windmills sprouted up on Color Island and many other islands and then on farms and in cities all over the world. People worked hard to plant new trees in the forests Eric and Ericka skied and hiked through, and then they began to plant more trees and make new forests. They grew new blueberry and other bushes. Some people started spending less time in cars and airplanes and more times in canoes or on bicycles or skis.

Eric the Skier

Did the people do enough? Did they do the right things? Did they do enough of them in time? No one knows for sure. People all over the world are worrying, not just Edwina. And many of those people are trying to do something about it, not just Edwina and Eric and the rest of their family. And that feels much better than doing nothing. It feels as good as Eric feels on his long yellow skis, and Eric knows how important it is—even more important than being a good skier.

After her family left, having waited twenty minutes while Edwina unlocked all thirty-three locks on her apartment door, Edwina started worrying again. But now she was thinking about things she would do and not just worrying. She still had a gray apartment, and it still had thirty-three locks on the door. Her cat was still named Worrywart, and it was still a gray cat. But now Edwina could get out from under her gray comforter, get on her colorful stationary bicycle, pretend she was with Eric or Alex or Erika and pedal some of her worries away with Worrywart in her arms. Now Edwina could be a healthier worrier. And she could remember her family and the wonderful birthday gift that brightened up her gray apartment.

Now Edwina knew that when she pedaled, she not only worried but thought about all the things she and her family and people she wrote to all over the world could do or already were doing. She knew it would be hard, very hard. Many people would have to work together. And they would have to work hard. They would have to learn many things, lessons from the past and research about the future. They would have to share their knowledge and ideas. They would have to plan carefully. There would be disappointments and mistakes. But they would have to keep going, just as Eric kept going on his long yellow skis no matter what happened. And while they worked together, they would be happier, just as Eric was always happy when he skied. They shouldn't be upset. They should just want to help. And every day they helped would make them feel like Eric starting out to ski across a new snowfield he had never seen before.

And now when Edwina pedaled, Worrywart forgot she was hungry and even purred from time to time before falling asleep in Edwina's arms. And Edwina hoped with all her heart that it was not too late to have a beautiful, healthy planet and that Eric on his long yellow skis would always be able to say, "It's a fin day for skiing." She knew in her heart that as long as everyone kept trying, they could all feel a little bit like Eric. As long as everyone kept trying.

Eric the Skier

About The Author

James B. Kobak, Jr., a largely retired lawyer, has previously written the Wimp's Guide to Cross-Country Skiing, the novel Up Front From Behind, and, most recently, Tennis, Anyone? The Wimp's Guide to Tennis and Other Racquet Sports. The last two were published by Humor Outcasts Press and the author is a contributor to the Humor Outcasts website as well as other publications. The book originated in stories he told his children, one of whom is the book's illustrator. Jim also posts essays, articles and poems from time to time on his substack, Jimkobak@substack.com.

www.ingramcontent.com/pod-product-compliance
Lightning Source LLC
Chambersburg PA
CBHW071121090426
42736CB00012B/1975